The past two decades have brought revolutionary changes in the understanding of the Indian civilization. This book written for the general reader presents an overview of this new understanding by a leading scholar and writer in the field. It is based on three invited lectures at Stanford University and the University of California on 14th and 15th April 2000.

Some comments on this work:

In *The Wishing Tree: Presence and Promise of India,* Subhash Kak presents what is arguably the most complete, articulate and up-to-date overview on the entire Indic tradition. More notably, he speaks not from a dry academic standpoint but from one in contact with the very soul and spirit of the culture. His panoramic view covers spirituality, science, linguistics and history, making clear India's important role in world civilization past, present and future. He dispels the many current distortions and misinterpretations of India, the cobwebs of colonial and Eurocentric thinking, and reveals her vast civilization in its true light. Everyone interested in India and in human civilization will be fascinated and transformed by his many-sided insights. They will never look at India again in the same way.

—David Frawley, author of *Gods, Sages and Kings* and other books

As a millennial retrospective of the trans-national journey of Indic ideas, *The Wishing Tree: Presence and Promise of India*, is an auspicious augury of a Cultural Renaissance among diaspora Indians. Subhash Kak's language is lucid; it is at times very poetic. His speaking voice is firm and precise. Reading this volume made me think that perhaps what is worth preserving in Indic traditions will endure the ravages of colonial/postcolonial fragmentation. Indic ideas are both secular and sacred, scientific and spiritual, utilitarian and unabashedly devoted to the principle of beauty. In his The *Wishing Tree*, Subhash Kak tells it all: with acuity, great insight and wisdom.

—Lalita Pandit, Professor of English, University of Wisconsin-La Crosse

Subhash Kak is a widely known scientist and Vedic scholar. Currently Head of the Computer Science Department at Oklahoma State University, he has authored seventeen books of which the most recent are *The Architecture of Knowledge* and *The Prajna Sutra*.

The Wishing Tree

The Wishing Tree

✦

Presence and Promise of India

Subhash Kak

Author of *The Gods Within*

iUniverse, Inc.

New York Bloomington Shanghai

The Wishing Tree
Presence and Promise of India

iUniverse books may be ordered through booksellers or by contacting:

iUniverse
1663 Liberty Drive
Bloomington, IN 47403
www.iuniverse.com
1-800-Authors (1-800-288-4677)

Because of the dynamic nature of the Internet, any Web addresses or links contained in this book may have changed since publication and may no longer be valid.

The views expressed in this work are solely those of the author and do not necessarily reflect the views of the publisher, and the publisher hereby disclaims any responsibility for them.

ISBN: 978-0-595-48699-1 (pbk)
ISBN: 978-0-595-49094-3 (cloth)
ISBN: 978-0-595-60796-9 (ebk)

Printed in the United States of America

Contents

Preface

The past two decades have brought revolutionary changes in our understanding of the Indian civilization. The chronology of the pre-historic period has been pushed back. Archaeologists tell us that the Indic civilization can be traced back in an unbroken sequence to at least 8000 BC. There is an even older rock art tradition that has been found all over India. Our understanding of the literature has also improved. Figures from the Vedas and the Puranas have started emerging into the historical narrative.

Although these findings are important in the self-definition of the Indian, they are being debated primarily in the pages of academic journals and at scholarly symposia. Many school textbooks and other popular books still repeat old, incorrect notions.

This essay, as an overview of this new understanding, is for the general reader. It is based on three invited lectures given at Stanford University and the Berkeley and Irvine campuses of the University of California. For this edition I have included new material related to India and the West that emerged out of a lecture given to the OHM Congress in the Hague.

Stillwater, Oklahoma, November 14, 2007   Subhash Kak

1
Introduction

What are the contributions of India to the world civilization? What does the latest research say about the antiquity of the Indian tradition? What relevance, if any, does India hold for the future? Can mainstream science benefit from Indic ideas? These are some of the questions I address in this little book.

In the imagination of the West, India is the land of magic and mystery, wisdom and religiosity, tradition and ritual. India is exotic; its arts, literature, music, cuisine appear different. But, at the same time, there are aspects to India that speak straight to the heart of the West.

This shouldn't surprise us because India and the West have had a shared prehistory. Sanskrit is the oldest remembered language of Asia and Europe. That the Indians and the Europeans shared the same homeland in remote antiquity has been the grist of ceaseless speculation. Indians are still connected to their past, which makes India a doorway for the discovery of the long-forgotten past of Europe.

But India appeals also because of its romance with the spirit. Indians have asked deep questions about our existence: Who are we? What is the nature of our inner self? They also claim to have found answers to these questions. The art historian and philosopher Heinrich Zimmer, put it thus: "We of the Occident are about to arrive at a crossroads that were reached by the thinkers of India some seven hundred years before Christ. That is the real reason why we become both vexed and stimulated, uneasy yet interested, when confronted with the concepts and images of Oriental wisdom."[1]

Columbus set out to find a new seaway to India and he ended up discovering America. Since then America and India have met in the realm of the spirit and, more recently, as partners in the development of information technology. In the 19th century, the Transcendentalists, inspired by Indian thought, gave a characteristic orientation to America's self-definition. Mohandas Gandhi was, in turn, influenced by Thoreau, one of the Transcendentalists, to embark on his *Satya-*

graha movement in South Africa and India. Half a century ago, Mohandas Gandhi's ideas influenced the civil rights movement in America. Most recently, Hindu wisdom about yoga, mind-body connection, and self-knowledge has swept the West. It appears that we are nearing the time when the quest of Columbus will be taken to its logical conclusion, to understanding the heart of the Indian civilization.

America is a country of great spaces and great appetites—both material and spiritual. The machines that are the foundation of America's material wealth compel conformity to their rhythms, leading to alienation, carpal tunnel syndrome, and angst about meaning. Americans are the most church-going nation of the world, but they are increasingly becoming aware of the limitations of organized religion and they seek psychologists and spiritual masters.

Indian spirituality, an unbroken sequence that goes back to hoary antiquity, holds a special fascination for the modern Westerner. It is a spirituality that is non-sectarian, universal and unconnected to ritual. Addressing the deepest questions of meaning and knowledge, it seems to speak to man's innermost concerns in this age of science.

Indian wisdom has been replenished for each generation by its epics, literature, fables, and aphorisms. India, with its ancient remembered past, is a counterpoint to an America whose history is no more than five hundred years old. The epics, literature, fables and aphorisms from the sacred and secular texts of India contain distilled wisdom. But the truths discovered by the sages of India will find resonance in America and the rest of the world not primarily through the literature but by its living traditions.

In India these traditions have been under relentless attack by colonialist and Marxists politicians and historians, who have controlled the public discourse and contents of the textbooks for nearly 200 years. The intention to destroy India's own traditions of knowledge was articulated in Macaulay's famous Minute of 1835 which led to the establishment of a colonialist system of education that is still in force. Macaulay justified this by saying, "I am quite ready to take the Oriental learning at the valuation of the Orientalists themselves. I have never found one among them who could deny that a single shelf of a good European library was worth the whole native literature of India … It is, I believe, no exaggeration to say, that all the historical information which has been collected from all the books written in the Sanscrit language is less valuable than what may be found in the most paltry abridgments used at preparatory schools in England … We must at present do our best to form a class who may be interpreters between us and the millions whom we govern; a class of persons, Indian in blood and colour, but English in taste, in opinions, in morals, and in intellect."[2]

Macaulay's ignorance about India was matched by his arrogance. His ideas were challenged in his own times, but they won the day because they suited Britain in its creation of a system which would make India dependent not only physically but also intellectually. Indian tradition was now interpreted for Indians by Western scholars ill-equipped to understand its complexity. Their synthesis cast Indian history in a mold that did it disservice. Indian civilization was called world-negating and mystical and shown as antithetical to the West.

Outside the halls of the ivory towers, the tradition was represented as being devoid of any real scientific achievement. The complexity of the social institutions was represented in the ill-fitting categories of hierarchical caste, and this, together with speculative philosophy, were declared to be the hallmarks of Indian civilization.

In practical terms, Macaulay's program led to the dismantling of the traditional system of village schools which had provided universal literacy to the people. The village schools had great room for improvement but they were very effective and were one of the institutions of local power. When they were superseded by new schools, run by the British bureaucracy using an alien language whose benefit ordinary people could not see, children of the poorer classes simply dropped out. This led to the great masses of the Indian population turning illiterate.

Central control was also disastrous for agriculture in many parts of the country where a system of tanks had existed for millennia. These tanks had been serviced by village councils. The English instituted a system of canal irrigation even where it was unsuitable and the local councils were disbanded. Soon, the tanks fell into disuse, the water table dropped because the ground water was not charged by the water in the tanks, and this had a ruinous effect on agriculture.

In the colonial state, the idea of profit was replaced by that of service of the British empire. The new system of education was instrumental in the socialization of this view. The idea of the other-worldly Indian was promoted.

Those, especially in the cities, who learned about India from these textbooks, soon came to hate their past. After independence, socialists seized control of institutions of education and the process set forth by the British was much accelerated. It is only now, sixty years after political independence, that an objective understanding of the foundations of Indian culture is beginning to emerge.

Those Indians, who have not internalized the imagined view of the Macaulayites, have always rejected it as false, because that is not how they saw themselves.

The Indian view has been to live life to the full, not only in body but also spirit. The essence of the Indian view is world-affirming and scientific.

Scholars have now found that a case can be made for the birth of the earliest geometry, mathematics, astronomy, medicine and many other sciences in India. In addition, India has had a very advanced tradition of contemplation and spiritual life.

2

A Bridge to the Future

There is a legend about a magic tree, *kalpataru,* that fulfills all wishes. Indian civilization is this tree of riches and wisdom. Kings and emperors sought to conquer India for its material wealth; the campaign of Alexander, the unceasing attacks of the Turks, the voyage of Columbus, the British empire—these had India as the focus. Indian sages, philosophers and mystics have held out a shining vision that has appealed to the world. Even Alexander took Indian yogis back to Greece with him.

Indian thought influenced not only China and Southeast Asia, it may also have provided key impulses to Western thought. We find the Indic people in West Asia in the second millennium BC in the Kassite kingdom of Babylon and the Mitannis of Syria. The father of the famous Queen Kiya of Egypt was the Mitanni king Tushratha (or Dasharatha). The Indic element has been seen in the beginnings of Greek art. It is quite conceivable that the religious traditions of West Asia preserve a remembrance of their Indic past.

The modern mind was shaped after adoption by the West of the twin beliefs of living in harmony with nature and search for a scientific basis to reality. In the past 300 years, these ideas of universality and a quest for knowledge have transformed European and American society. Many of the greatest writers and scientists of the past 100 years have taken inspiration from these Indic ideas.

Erwin Schrödinger

Perhaps the most remarkable intellectual achievement of the twentieth century was quantum theory, which is at the basis of our understanding of chemistry, biology, and physics and, consequently, it is at the basis of the century's astonishing technological advances. One of the two creators of this theory was Erwin Schrödinger (1887-1961). In an autobiographical essay, he explains that his discovery of quantum mechanics was an attempt to give form to central ideas of

Vedanta which, in this indirect sense, has played a role in the birth of the subject. In 1925, *before* his revolutionary theory was complete, Erwin Schrödinger wrote:

> This life of yours which you are living is not merely a piece of this entire existence, but in a certain sense the whole; only this whole is not so constituted that it can be surveyed in one single glance. This, as we know, is what the Brahmins express in that sacred, mystic formula which is yet really so simple and so clear: *tat tvam asi*, this is you. Or, again, in such words as "I am in the east and the west, I am above and below, *I am this entire world.*"[3]

Schrödinger's influential *What is Life?* (1944) also used Vedic ideas. The book became instantly famous although it was criticized by some for its emphasis on Indian ideas. Francis Crick, the co-discoverer of the DNA code, credited this book for key insights that led him to his revolutionary discovery.

According to his biographer Walter Moore, there is a clear continuity between Schrödinger's understanding of Vedanta and his research:

> The unity and continuity of Vedanta are reflected in the unity and continuity of wave mechanics. In 1925, the world view of physics was a model of a great machine composed of separable interacting material particles. During the next few years, Schrödinger and Heisenberg and their followers created a universe based on superimposed inseparable waves of probability amplitudes. This new view would be entirely consistent with the Vedantic concept of *All in One.*[4]

He became a Vedantist, a Hindu, as a result of his studies in his search for truth. Schrödinger kept a copy of the Hindu scriptures at his bedside. He read books on Vedas, yoga, and Sankhya philosophy and he reworked them into his own words, and ultimately came to believe them. The Upanishads and the Bhagavadgita were his favourite scriptures.

According to his biographer Moore, "His system—or that of the Upanishads—is delightful and consistent: the self and the world are one and they are all. He rejected traditional western religious beliefs (Jewish, Christian, and Islamic) not on the basis of any reasoned argument, nor even with an expression of emotional antipathy, for he loved to use religious expressions and metaphors, but simply by saying that they are naive."[5]

Schrödinger was a professor at several universities in Europe. He was awarded the Nobel Prize in 1933. During the Hitler era he was dismissed from his position for his opposition to the Nazi ideas and he fled to England. For some years he was in Ireland, but after the conclusion of the World War II he returned to Vienna where he died in 1961.

Quantum mechanics goes beyond ordinary logic. According to it reality is a superposition of all possibilities which is very different from classical physics. It is quantum mechanics which explains the mysteries of chemical reactions and of life. In recent years, it has been suggested that the secrets of consciousness have a quantum basis.

In a famous essay on determinism and free will, Schrödinger expressed very clearly the sense that consciousness is a unity, arguing that this "insight is not new … From the early great Upanishads the recognition *Atman* = *Brahman* (the personal self equals the omnipresent, all-comprehending eternal self) was in Indian thought considered, far from being blasphemous, to represent the quintessence of deepest insight into the happenings of the world. The striving of all the scholars of Vedanta was, after having learnt to pronounce with their lips, really to assimilate in their minds this grandest of all thoughts."[6]

He thought the idea of pluralization of consciousness and the notion of many souls to be naive. He considered the notion of plurality to be a result of deception (*maya*): "the same illusion is produced by a gallery of mirrors, and in the same way Gaurisankar and Mt. Everest turned out to be the same peak seen from different valleys."[7]

Schrödinger was a very complex person. But he had a sense of humor and paradox. He called his dog *Atman*. Perhaps he did this to honour Yudhishthira whose own dog, an incarnation of cosmic justice (Dharma), accompanied him on his last march to the Himalayas. More likely, he was calling attention to the unity that pervades the web of life.

Changing Understanding

There are several reasons for us to be interested in India. Some relate to the past to the origins of science and religion, others concern our yearning for knowledge of self and future of mankind. The Indian culture area provides us extensive material, across a very broad time-span, to help us understand some of the earliest history of ideas. The ancient Indian texts are layered in such a fashion that we can see the gradual development of mathematical, physical, linguistic, and psychological ideas. We find that the ancient Indians were greatly interested in geometry, astronomy, grammar, music and other fields. They were also interested in cognitive science where they were so advanced that their insights may yet be useful to modern science.

The understanding of the chronological framework of the Indian civilization has changed greatly in the last few years due to revolutionary discoveries in archaeology. The archaeological record has been traced in an unbroken tradition to about 8000 BC. The earliest textual source is the Rigveda, a compilation of very early material. There are astronomical references in this and the other Vedic books which recall events in the third to the fifth millennium BC and earlier. The recent discovery that Sarasvati, the preeminent river of the Rigvedic times, went dry around 1900 BC due to tectonic upheavals implies that the Rigveda is to be dated prior to this epoch. According to traditional history, the Rigveda is prior to 3100 BC.[8]

There is difference in the nature of the community and state in this tradition and the civilizations of West Asia. The West has monumental temples, tombs, palaces whereas the society in India appears to have been governed by a sacred order.

The beginning of Indian writing has been traced to about 3300 BC in marks on potsherds. More extensive seals and inscriptions date to 2600 BC onwards. The original writing should perhaps be called Sarasvati (because its main provenance was the Sarasvati valley region), and it is this that was given the name the Indus script in the last century, when inscriptions in this writing were unearthed.

The later historical script called Brahmi evolved out of the Indus-Sarasvati writing. The earliest records of Brahmi have been traced to 500 BC or so in Sri Lanka, but clearly it must have been in use for a long, long time before that. All the modern Indic and Southeast Asian scripts are derived from Brahmi. The invention of the symbol for zero appears to have been made around 50 BC to 50 AD.

The earliest Indic art is preserved on rocks in the paleolithic, mesolithic and neolithic stages and the seals and the sculpture of the Indus-Sarasvati phase which lasted from about 8000 BC to 1900 BC. The beginnings of the rock art have been traced to 40,000 years BP (before present) in the decorated ostrich eggshells from Rajasthan; its dating is based on radiocarbon techniques. Subsequent phases have been determined using evolution of style and other radiocarbon dates. The mesolithic period has been dated as 12000 to 6000 BP. The sites of the rock are found distributed all over the country, with the most impressive sites located in Madhya Pradesh.[9]

The earliest drawings of rock art tradition are characterized by dynamic action, vitality in form, and an acute insight into abstraction and visual perception. It has been found that there is significant continuity of motif in the rock art and the later Indus-Sarasvati civilization indicating an unbroken link with the paleolithic and the mesolithic cultures of India. A striking aspect of the early rock art is its drawing of tessellations, which show infinite repetition. This repetition may occur for a basic pattern or, more abstractly, the lines extend spatially in a manner so that a basic pattern is repeated in two directions. An understanding of this abstract concept must have been a part of the thought system of the artists. This reminds us of the central place of the notion of infinite in later Indian thought.

The abstract and the iconic elements in Indian rock art are unique. They are different from the more naturalistic ancient European cave paintings.

One aspect of the Indian literary tradition, which is several thousand years old, is its speculative imagination. The epic Mahabharata mentions embryo transplantation, multiple births from the same fetus, battle with extra-terrestrials who are wearing air-tight suits, and weapons of mass-destruction. The Ramayana mentions air travel. The Bhagavata Purana, a medieval encyclopaedic text, has episodes related to different passage of time for different observers that are very similar to what happens in the theory of relativity. The notion of self in the Upanishads embodies a very subtle understanding of observers and of reality. The Yoga Vasishtha and the Tripura Rahasya present a deep discussion of the nature of consciousness. This is unique to the Indic civilization. Does it mean that the Indian belief that synthetic knowledge itself could be obtained by the mind may not be all that outrageous?

Time Periods

The chronology of Indian culture has been a subject of some dispute. According to tradition, the Vedic period ended about 5,000 years ago. But the evidence from the Vedic texts itself is peripheral to this question and that from the Puranas is not always consistent.

The modern science of archaeology, using radio-carbon and other dating techniques, has helped in forming an outline of the different stages of cultural and material development.

The archaeological periods are:

1.   Rock Art Period: 40,000 BC onwards to historical times

2.   The Indus-Sarasvati Tradition: 8000 BC to 1300 BC

3.   Early Harappan: 3300 BC to 2600 BC

4.   The mature Harappan period: 2600 BC to 1900 BC

5. Late Harappan: 1900 BC to 1300 BC

6. Regionalization period (Painted Grey Ware): 1300 BC to 800 BC

7. Northern Black Polished Ware: 800 BC to 500 BC

This takes us to the period of Gautama Buddha and the classical period of Indian art and architecture.

The Puranic genealogies start with mythical events and the early Saptarshi calendar starts from the epoch of 6676 BC which is taken to be the beginning of the genealogies; a later Saptarshi calendar, still in use in different parts of the country, begins from 3076 BC. Other old calendars are Kaliyuga (3102 BC), Vikrama (58 BC), Shaka (78 AD).

The Mahabharata War was the epochal event of ancient India. Later astronomers assigned it to 3137 BC or 2449 BC. Still other traditions assign it to 1924 BC or about 1500 BC. The main actors of this War belong to generation number 94 in a list that is supposed to begin in 6676 BC. Clearly, if the genealogies are genuine, they cannot be complete. In all likelihood, they only speak of the most important kings. It is possible that the beginning of 6676 BC was arrived at by some backdating. Nevertheless, there is considerable evidence that the genealogies represent a very ancient tradition.

The early Indian Sanskrit literature falls in the following main layers:

- The Vedic collections: pre-2000 BC by the Sarasvati river argument. Traditionally assigned the period pre-3000 BC.

- The Brahmanas (prose commentaries on the Vedas): 1900–1600 BC, because they speak of the drying up of Sarasvati river as a recent happening.

- The Aranyakas (forest books): 1500–1200 BC, this period followed the Brahmanas.

- The Upanishads (wisdom books): 1900–1000 BC appears to be the period of the earliest Upanishads. The Bhagavadgita appears to belong to the end of this period.

- The Sutras (aphoristic books): These were written in the centuries before and after the Buddha.

- The Puranas. The original Purana was coterminous with the Vedas, but this later gave rise to several texts. The Puranas are encyclopaedias of Vedic mythology and spirituality.

- The Mahabharata and the Ramayana. The original Mahabharata dates to the Mahabharata War. A series of enlargements made it attain its size of 100,000 verses about two thousand five hundred years ago. The Ramayana is an epic poem that deals with events earlier than those of the Mahabharata.

This is a bare chronological frame based on much guesswork, and we don't know how to fit in specific texts with certainty within it. Even more difficult is the assignment of dates to ancient kings and sages. But it is such a long period that we can understand how by the time of the Buddha, Vedic ritual had become unintelligible to most people.

Genetic Evidence

In an important book titled *The Real Eve: Modern Man's Journey out of Africa*,[10] the prominent Oxford University scholar Stephen Oppenheimer has synthesized the available genetic evidence together with climatology and archeology with conclusions which have bearing on the debate about the early population of India.

Much of Oppenheimer's theory is based on recent advances in studies of mitochondrial DNA, inherited through the mother, and Y chromosomes, inherited by males from the father. Oppenheimer makes the case that whereas Africa is the cradle of all mankind; India is the cradle of all non-African peoples. Man left Africa approximately 90,000 years ago, heading east along the Indian Ocean, and established settlements in India. It was only during a break in glacial activity 50,000 years ago, when deserts turned into grasslands, that people left India and headed northwest into the Russian steppes and on into Eastern Europe, as well as northeast through China and over the now submerged Bering Strait into the Americas.

In their migration to India, African people carried the mitochondrial DNA strain L3 and Y chromosome line M168 across south Red sea across the southern part of the Arabian Peninsula. On the maternal side the mtDNA strain L3 split into two daughters which Oppenheimer labels Nasreen and Manju. While Manju was definitely born in India the birthplace of Nasreen is tentatively placed by him in southern Iran or Baluchistan. One Indian Manju subclan in India is as old as 73,000 years, whereas European man goes back to less than 50,000 years.

Considering the paternal side, Oppenheimer sees M168 as having three sons, of whom Seth was the most important one. Seth, in turn, had five sons which are named by him as Jahangir, H, I, G and Krishna. Krishna, born in India, is the ancestor of the peoples of East Asia, Central Asia, Oceania and West Eurasia (through the M17 mutation). This is what Oppenheimer says about M17:

> South Asia is logically the ultimate origin of M17 and his ancestors; and sure enough we find highest rates and greatest diversity of the M17 line in Pakistan, India, and eastern Iran, and low rates in the Caucasus. M17 is not only more diverse in South Asia than in Central Asia but diversity characterizes its presence in isolated tribal groups in the south, thus undermining any theory of M17 as a marker of a "male Aryan Invasion of India." (page 152)
>
> Study of the geographical distribution and the diversity of genetic branches and stems again suggests that Ruslan, along with his son M17, arose early in South Asia, somewhere near India, and subsequently spread not only southeast to Australia but also north, directly to Central Asia, before splitting east and west into Europe and East Asia. (page 153)

Oppenheimer argues that the Eurocentric view of ancient history is also incorrect. For example, Europeans didn't invent art, because the Australian aborigines developed their own unique artistic culture in complete isolation. Indian rock art is also extremely ancient, going back to over 40,000 BC, so perhaps art as a part of culture had arisen in Africa itself. Similarly, agriculture didn't arise in the Fertile Crescent; Southeast Asia had already domesticated many plants by that time.

Oppenheimer concludes with two extraordinary conclusions: "First, that the Europeans' genetic homeland was originally in South Asia in the Pakistan/Gulf region over 50,000 years ago; and second, that the Europeans' ancestors followed at least two widely separated routes to arrive, ultimately, in the same cold but rich garden. The earliest of these routes was the Fertile Crescent. The second early route from South Asia to Europe may have been up the Indus into Kashmir and on to Central Asia, where perhaps more than 40,000 years ago hunters first started bringing down game as large as mammoths." (pp. 153-154)

This synthesis of genetic evidence makes it possible to understand the divide between the north and the south Indian languages. It appears that the Dravidian languages are more ancient, and the Aryan languages *evolved in India* over thousands of years before migrations took them to central Asia and westward to Europe. The proto-Dravidian languages had also, through the ocean route, reached northeast Asia, explaining the connections between the Dravidian family and the Korean and the Japanese.

3

Language Wars

The chronological frame sketched in the previous chapter is somewhat different from the dogma of the generation past. Then we were told that India was invaded around 1500 BC by Aryans from Central Asia or, perhaps, even South Europe. This dogma was at the basis of the construction of an elaborate scenario related to strife between the speakers of the Aryan and Dravidian languages.

As the science of language, historical linguistics in the early 19th century saw itself as providing a framework for studying the history and relationships of languages in the same manner as biology describes the animal world. But whereas biology has been revolutionized by the discovery of the genetic code, no similar breakthrough has brought new illumination to linguistics. Over the protestations of its many critics, mainstream historical linguistics has remained within the parameters of 19th century thinking. In the meanwhile, archaeological discoveries have altered our understanding of ancient Eurasia. The Indo-Europeans are seen to be present in Europe a few thousand years earlier than was supposed before. The Indian evidence, based on archaeology as well as the discovery of an astronomy in the Vedas, indicates that Vedic Sanskrit is to be assigned to the 4th and the 3rd millennia BC, if not earlier. The Indian cultural area is seen as an integral whole. The Vedic texts are being interpreted as a record of the complex transformations taking place in the pre-2000 BC Indian society.

We understand how the 19th century construction of the Orient by the West satisfied its needs of self-definition in relation to the Other. To justify its ascendancy, the Other was defined to be racially mixed and inferior, irrational and primitive, despotic and feudal. This definition was facilitated by a selective use of the texts and rejecting traditional interpretations, an approach that is now called Orientalism. The terms in the construction were not properly defined. Now we know that to speak of a "pure" race is meaningless since all external characteristics of humans are defined in a continuum. In the 19th century atmosphere of European triumphalism, what was obtained in Europe was taken to be normative.

With hindsight it is hard to believe that these ideas were not contested more vigorously.

Although this was the age that marked the true beginnings of modern science, old myths continued to exercise great power. When it was found that the languages of India and Europe were related in structure and vocabulary, the West responded with what J.-P. Vernant calls "a tissue of scholarly myths. These myths were steeped in erudition, informed by profound knowledge of Hebrew and Sanskrit, fortified by comparative study of linguistic data, mythology, and religion, and shaped by the effort to relate linguistic structures, forms of thought, and features of civilization. Yet they were also myths, fantasies of the social imagination, at every level. The comparative philology of the most ancient languages was a quest for origins, an attempt to return to a privileged moment in time when God, man, and natural forces still lived in mutual transparency. The plunge into the distant past in search of 'roots' went hand in hand with a never forgotten faith in a meaningful history, whose course, guided by the Providence of the one God, could be understood only in the light of Christian revelation. As scholars established the disciplines of Semitic and Indo-European studies, they also invented the mythical figures of the Hebrew and the Aryan, a providential pair which, by revealing to the people of the Christianized West the secret of their identity, also bestowed upon them the patent of nobility that justified their spiritual, religious, and political domination of the world."[11]

Although the term Aryan never had a racial connotation in the Indian texts, the scholars insisted that this was the sense in which the term ought to be understood. It was further assumed that Aryan meant European by race. By doing so Europe claimed for itself all of the "Aryan" texts as a part of its own forgotten past.

The West considered itself the inheritor of the imagination and the mythic past of the Aryan and the idea of the monotheism of the Hebrew. This dual inheritance was the mark of the imperial destiny of the West. Vernant reminds us that despite his monotheism, the poor Jew, since he lacked Aryan blood, should have seen "the dark silhouette of the death camps and the rising smoke of the ovens."[12]

On the other hand, the Asiatic mixed-blood Aryan had no future but that of the serf. He could somewhat redeem himself if he rejected all but the earliest core of his inheritance, that existed when the Aryans in India were a pure race. For scholars such as Max Müller this became ultimately a religious issue. Echoing Augustine, Müller saw in his own religious faith a way for progress of the Asiatic. We would smile at it now but he said, "Christianity was simply the name 'of the true religion,' a religion that was already known to the ancients and indeed had been around 'since the beginning of the human race.'"[13] But ideas—bad and good—never die. Müller's idea has recently been resurrected in the guise that Christianity is the fulfillment of Vedic revelation!

A linguistic "Garden of Eden" called the proto-Indo-European (PIE) language was postulated. Europe was taken to be the homeland of this language for which several wonderful qualities were assumed. This was a theory of race linking the Europeans to the inhabitants of the original homeland and declaring them to be original speakers of the PIE. By appropriating the origins, the Europeans also appropriated the oldest literature of the Indians and of other IE speakers. Without a past how could the nations of the empire ever aspire to equality with the West?

Indian literature was seen to belong to two distinct layers. At the deepest level were the Vedas that represented the outpourings of the nature-worshiping pure Aryans. At the next level, weakened by an admixture with the indigenous tribes, the literature became a narrative on irrational ritual.

Science and Pseudoscience

In scientific or rational discourse the empirical data can, in principle, falsify a theory. This is why creationism, which explains the fossil record as well as evolution by assuming that it was placed there along with everything else by God when he created the universe in 4004 BC, is not a scientific theory: creationism is unfalsifiable. Building a scientific theory one must also use the Occam's razor, according to which the most economical hypothesis that explains the data is to be accepted.

Bad intent should not turn anyone away from good science. Why isn't PIE good science? It looks reasonable enough: If there are biological origins then there should be linguistic origins as well. And why don't we believe that the nature of language tells us something about culture? If Europeans have been dominant in recent history, then why don't we accept it as a characteristic of the European? Thus the origin of the PIE must be in the European sphere from where the energy of its early speakers carried them to the far corners of Asia and allowed them to impose their language on the native speakers.

There are several problems with the idea of PIE. It is based on the hypothesis that languages are defined as fixed entities and they evolve in a biological sense. In reality, a language area is a complex, graded system of several languages and dialects of a family. The degree of homogeneity in a language area is a reflection of the linkages, or interaction within the area. For a language distributed widely in the ancient world, one would expect several dialects. There would be no standard proto-language.

It is clear that language families belong to overlapping groups, because such a view allows us to represent better the complex history of the interactions amongst their ancestor languages. Such an overlap need not imply that the speakers of either group intruded into the overlapping region.

We note further the warning by N.S. Trubetskoy (1939) that the presence of the same word in a number of languages need not suggest that these languages descended from a common parent:[14]

> There is, then, no powerful ground for the assumption of a unitary Indoger-man protolanguage, from which the individual Indogerman language groups would derive. It is just as plausible that the ancestors of the Indogerman lan-guage groups were originally quite dissimilar, and that through continuing contact, mutual influence and word borrowing became significantly closer to each other, without however going so far as to become identical.

The evolution of a language with time is a process governed by context-sensi-tive rules that express the complex history of interactions with different groups over centuries. The changes in each region will reflect the interaction of the speakers with the speakers of other languages (most of which are now extinct) and various patterns of bilingualism.

There is no evidence that can prove or disprove an original language such as PIE. We cannot infer it with certainty since the historically attested relationship between different languages could have emerged from one of many competing models. If one considers the situation that prevailed in the New World when Europeans arrived as typical, the ancient Old World had a multitude of lan-guages. It is from this great language diversity that a process akin to biological extinction led to the currently much smaller family of languages. Scholars now say that the metaphor of a perfect or pure language leading to large diversity must be replaced by the metaphor of a web. This becomes clear when we consider bio-logical inheritance. We inherit our genes from more than one ancestor.

The postulation of PIE together with a specific homeland in Europe or Tur-key does violence to facts. There is no evidence that the natives of India for the past 8,000 years or so have looked any different from what they look now. The internal evidence of this literature points to events that are as early as 7000 years ago and its geography is squarely in the Indian region.

If there was no single PIE, there was no single homeland either. The postula-tion of an "original home", without anchoring it to a definite time-period is to fall in the same logical trap as in the search for invasions and immigration. Tree or animal name evidence cannot fix a homeland. In a web of languages, different geographical areas will indicate tree or animal names that are specific to these areas. When the European side of the IE languages is examined, the tree or animal names will favour those found in its climate and when the Indian side of the languages are examined, the reference now will be to its flora and fauna.

Colin Renfrew has pointed out how a circular logic has been used by linguists to justify what has already been implicit in their assumptions. Speaking of the work by Paul Friedrich (1970) on "Proto-Indo-European trees", Renfrew reminds us that the starting assumption there is that PIE was current in western Caspian and the Carpathians during the fourth millennium and the first centuries of the third millennium and then Friedrich proves that this was the PIE homeland! Reminds Renfrew:[15]

> [Friedrich's] assumption is highly questionable. So complete an adoption of one specific solution to the question of Indo-European origins is bound to have a considerable impact upon his analysis of the origins of tree-names, and the historical conclusions he reaches. It is scarcely surprising if his theory harmonizes with the historical reconstruction upon which it is based. It is perhaps reasonable that the historical linguistics should be based upon the archaeology, but that the archaeological interpretation should simultaneously be based upon the linguistic analysis gives serious cause for concern. Each discipline assumes that the other can offer conclusions based upon sound independent evidence, but in reality one begins where the other ends. They are both relying on each other to prop up their mutual thesis.

Aryan and Dravidian

It was Bishop Caldwell (1875) who suggested that the South Indian languages of Tamil, Malayalam, Kannada, and Telugu formed the separate Dravidian family of languages. He further suggested that the speakers of the proto-Dravidian language entered India from the northwest. Other scholars argued against this Dravidian invasion theory. Scholars have argued that this attempt to see both the North and the South Indian languages coming to the subcontinent from outside (West Asia) as another example of the preoccupation with the notion of the "Garden of Eden". In reality, the problem of what constitutes an Aryan or a Dravidian, in the biological or cultural sense in which it is generally posed, is insoluble.

The problem of Aryan and Dravidian is a conflation of many categories. Indian texts do not use the term Arya or Aryan in a linguistic sense, only in terms of culture. There is reference in the Manu Smriti where even the Chinese are termed Aryan, proving that it is not the language that defines this term. The South Indian kings called themselves Aryan as did the South Indian travelers who took Indian civilization to Southeast Asia.

One may have posed the problem in terms of the anthropological "distinction" between the speaker of the North and the South Indian languages. But the anthropologists tell us that there is no difference.

When linguists in the last century insisted that the term "Aryan" be reserved for the North Indian languages alone, it was inevitable confusion would emerge.

The definition of Aryan and Dravidian are extrapolated from the culture of the speakers of the North and the South Indian languages. But the cultures of the North and the South are the same as far back as we can go. (There is some minor difference in kinship rules.)

There is even a mirroring of the sacred geography. The North has Kashi and Mathura; the South has Kanchi and Madurai. Who is to say what the original was? If there is no cultural difference then the use of the term "Aryan" as defining the culture of just the speakers of the North Indian languages is misleading.

This following example puts the absurdity of the terminology in focus. There exist texts that state that Tamilian Hindus came and settled in Kashmir in the early 15th century in the liberal reign of Bada Shah. We don't know how many people came, but that is the nature of such textual evidence anyway. Now what does that make a Kashmiri? An Aryan or a Dravidian?

Some scholars have claimed a Dravidian substratum for Marathi, but how do we know that prior to that Dravidian substratum there was not some other language that was spoken there? And maybe there has been more than one shift back and forth.

Let's imagine that everyone in India originally spoke Dravidian and then due to some process of "elite dominance" most people in the North started speaking Indo-Aryan and they kept their old traditions and legends. The new speakers will still be culturally Dravidian and certainly they would be so "biologically", if that could ever mean anything. If this is what happened in India then are the Aryans actually Dravidians and, by implication, are the Dravidians also Aryans? There could be two groups of people speaking two different languages who culturally belong to the same tradition like the modern-day Hungarians and Czechs.

We don't know who the authors of the Vedas were. They could have been bilingual speakers who knew "Dravidian" and "Vedic"; maybe their first language was really Dravidian even though they had Sanskrit names as has been true in

South India for much of historical times; or they were purely Sanskrit speaking. No rhetoric or ideology can resolve this question.

The use of a language in literature does not even mean that the speakers are a dominant elite. Let's consider the use of Urdu in Pakistan. The Punjabi speaking Punjabis are the dominant group but Urdu is used for official work purely due to some historical factors. In fact, the only Urdu-speaking ethnic group in Pakistan, the Mohajirs, feel they are at the bottom of the totem pole.

The texts cannot reveal the ethnic background just as Indians in the US who have adopted American names cannot be identified as ethnically Indian from their writing. The lesson is that the term "Aryan", misused by so many different parties, should be retired from academic discourse.

Several Kinds of Families

The Indian linguistic evidence requires the postulation of two kinds of classification. The first is the traditional Indian classification where the whole of India is a single linguistic area of what used to be traditionally called the Prakrit family. Linguists agree that based on certain structural relationships the North and the South Indian languages are closer than Sanskrit and Greek.[16]

Second, we have a division between the North Indian languages that should really be called North Prakrit (called Indo-Aryan by the linguists) and the South Indian languages that may be called South Prakrit (or Dravidian).

There is also the Indo-European family to which the North Prakrit languages belong. Likewise, Dravidian has been assumed to belong to a larger family of agglutinative languages.

This classification will allow us to get rid of the term Aryan in marking the families of languages, allowing us to move past the racist connotation behind its 19th century use. Its further virtue is that it recognizes that language families cannot be exclusive systems and they should be perceived as overlapping circles that expand and shrink with time.

Back to the Origins

Some Indologists driven by the old race paradigm have stood facts upside down to force them to fit their theory. We know that the internal evidence of the Indian texts shows that the Vedas precede the Puranas. Since Puranic themes occur in the iconography of the Harappan times (2600-1900 BC), some take the Puranic material to precede the Vedas so that the Vedas could be placed in the second millennium BC.

I think the only logical resolution of all the archaeological and textual evidence is to assume that the Indic area became a single cultural area at least around 5000 BC. The Indian civilization was created by the speakers of many languages but the language of the earliest surviving literary expression was Vedic Sanskrit, that is itself connected to both the North and the South Prakrit languages.

This idea is supported not only by the internal evidence that shows that the Indic tradition from 7000 BC onwards is an indigenous affair, but also from the new analysis of ancient art. For example, David Napier argues that the forehead markings of the Gorgon and the single-eye of the cyclops in Greek art are Indian elements. Although he suggests that this may have been a byproduct of the interaction with the Indian foot soldiers who fought for the Persian armies, he doesn't fail to mention the more likely possibility that the influence was through the 2nd millennium BC South Indian traders in Greece. This is supported by the fact that the name of the Mycenaean Greek city Tiryns—the place where the most ancient monuments of Greece are to be found—is the same as that of the most powerful Tamilian sea-faring people called the Tirayans.[17]

Since the 2nd millennium interaction between Greece and India is becoming clear only now, it is appropriate to ask if our languages were frozen into fixed categories wrongly by the 19th century historical linguists.

Consider the *centum/satem* divide in which European languages belong to the *centum* group and the North Indian languages to the *satem* group. The tree model is used to divide the PIE into these two sub-classes with the *centum* group representing the western branch and the *satem* group representing the eastern branch. The discovery of Tocharian as a *centum* language was seen as an example of a heroic movement of *centum*-speaking people from the west. But now the discovery of Bangani, a *centum* language in India, has make the whole idea of a tree-like division suspect.

Consider also the question of our knowledge of the vocabulary of various languages. For some languages, this knowledge was primarily obtained in quick field-work done decades ago by scholars who were not native speakers. Could it be that they missed out on vital evidence?

One of the orthodox scholars informs us[18] that the word *mori* "seems originally to have meant swamp, marsh land or lake, rather than a large body of open water. [I]t is found only in European languages and not in Indo-Iranian other than Ossetic—an Iranian language contiguous to Europe although originating further to the east." This "fact" has lent itself to endless theorizing. But this "fact" is a result of incomplete surveys. The word *mar*, a cognate, is a common Kashmiri term for a swamp or even a lake. We see this word in the formation of

Kashyapmar from which the word Kashmir is derived. Even Kannada has a cognate.

Also, many Hindi speakers pronounce the word for "hundred" as *sainkara* rather than *saikara*, which the field studies tell us is the "correct" form. Does that make Hindi a *centum* language?

The archaeological findings from India and the discovery of the astronomy of the Vedic period are fatal for the constructions of historical linguistics that arose in the 19th century and are still being followed in schoolbooks in India although textbooks in the West have begun to present the new picture. While the general language categories seem reasonable, the concept of overlapping families seems essential to obtain better conceptual clarity.

The breakdown of the old paradigm calls for considerable effort to create a new one to take its place. In particular, the emerging chronological framework can be used to examine the relationships between Sanskrit and other ancient Indo-European languages. Etymological dictionaries should be revised to take note of the antiquity of Vedic Sanskrit. If PIE did not exist, can we extrapolate from the earliest layer of Vedic Sanskrit for correlations with life in prehistoric Harappan India?

4

The Myth of Aryan Invasions

In talking of the past we must remember that our narratives are scraps of evidence joined with the glue of imagination. So there can be many narratives and many retellings as the vocabulary changes with time. This is all ancient history can be and we should be satisfied with that. It is sensible to accept that our reconstructions of the past are subjective.

But what does one do if a narrative is at variance with the evidence and yet, because of endless repetition, it has become entrenched in popular imagination as well as scholarly discourse? And what if such a narrative is accepted as the only truth?

Here I am talking of the fabrication of the narrative of Aryan invasions of the 2nd millennium BC. All evidence we have goes against it: There is biological continuity in the skeletal record for 4500-800 BC; the archaeological record belongs to the same cultural tradition from 8000 BC to historical times; the literary texts know of no other geography but that of India; and so on.

Even the horses supposedly used by the Central Asian Aryan invaders are a different kind from the ones described in the Vedic books. The Central Asian horse has 18 pairs of ribs, while the horse described in the Vedic books has only 17 pairs. Neither was cattle brought here by the *cattle-obsessed* Aryans looking for fresh grazing grounds for their animals. Analysis of the genetic make-up of the Indian zebu population and the taurine animals in Africa and Europe shows they are different, providing strong support for the hypothesis that these cattle were domesticated independently by two different Neolithic cultures. Similar analyses show that the Middle Eastern populations gave rise to European cattle.

Furthermore, the texts remember several astronomical events that took place during 5000 BC to 1000 BC; they also state that the Sarasvati flowed to the sea, which is memory of a period prior to 1900 BC, because we now know that the river dried up around that time. Here it is not my intention to review the evidence for which broad consensus exists amongst archaeologists.

So what should we do if some textbooks continue to repeat this fabrication? There are those who say that history doesn't matter and so let's not worry about what the books say and in due course better books will be published.

Maybe so. But isn't it foolish to let wrong things be taught in schools and colleges? How does it help education if we assault the intelligence of the youth and tell them something to be a fact for which there is no evidence?

It is bad enough if a fabrication—a story—is palmed off as the truth, but what if the fabrication is driven not just by poor logic but by racism?

Ten years ago, the distinguished British anthropologist, Edmund Leach, wrote a famous essay on this problem titled "Aryan Invasions Over Four Millennia." Published in a book called *Culture Through Time* (edited by Emiko Ohnuki-Tierney, Stanford University Press, 1990), this essay exposed the racist basis of the 19th century construction of Indian prehistory and, perhaps more important for us, it showed how racism persists in the academic approach to the study of India. The implication of Leach's charge is that many of the assumptions at the basis of the academic study of Indian social organization, language development, and evolution of religion are simply wrong! Here are some excerpts from this essay:[19]

> Why do serious scholars persist in believing in the Aryan invasions? … Why is this sort of thing attractive? Who finds it attractive? Why has the development of early Sanskrit come to be so dogmatically associated with an Aryan invasion? …
>
> Where the Indo-European philologists are concerned, the invasion argument is tied in with their assumption that if a particular language is identified as having been used in a particular locality at a particular time, no attention need be paid to what was there before; the slate is wiped clean. Obviously, the easiest way to imagine this happening in real life is to have a military conquest that obliterates the previously existing population!
>
> The details of the theory fit in with this racist framework … Because of their commitment to a unilineal segmentary history of language development that needed to be mapped onto the ground, the philologists took it for granted that proto-Indo-Iranian was a language that had originated outside either India or Iran. Hence it followed that the text of the Rig Veda was in a language that was actually spoken by those who introduced this earliest form of Sanskrit into India. From this we derived the myth of the Aryan invasions. QED.
>
> The origin myth of British colonial imperialism helped the elite administrators in the Indian Civil Service to see themselves as bringing 'pure' civilization to a country in which civilization of the most sophisticated (but 'morally corrupt') kind was already nearly 6,000 years old. Here I will only remark that

the hold of this myth on the British middle-class imagination is so strong that even today, 44 years after the death of Hitler and 43 years after the creation of an independent India and independent Pakistan, the Aryan invasions of the second millennium BC are still treated as if they were an established fact of history.

In editorial comments, Ohnuki-Tierney summarizes Leach's arguments regarding the fabrication: "Seemingly objective academic endeavors are affected by the mentalite of the culture to which they belong. Leach describes how cherished but erroneous assumptions in linguistics and anthropology wre accepted without question. If the mentalite of the academic culture was in part responsible for the fabrication, geopolitics was even more responsible for upholding the Aryan invasion as history. The theory fit the Western or British vision of their place in the world at the time. The conquest of Asian civilization needed a mythical charter to serve as the moral justification for colonial expansion. Convenient, if not consciously acknowledged, was the Aryan invasion by a fair-skinned people, speaking the so-called Proto-Indo-European language, militarily conquering the dark-skinned, peasant Dasa (Dasyu), who spoke a non-European language and with whom the conquerors lived, as Leach puts it, in a 'system of sexual apartheid.' ... A remarkable case of Orientalism indeed."[20]

The Hegemonic Circle

According to the postmodern theorist Lalita Pandit conventions of history writing are more often than not marked by intellectual bad faith that serves and maintains hegemonic ideologies. She adds, "it is nearly impossible to alter the premises of hegemonic claims, because hegemonies are founded in such retellings, and passing off of myth for fact and history, non-truth for belief. In part at least, all hegemonies are founded in discourses. Discourse conventions are automatically set to deal with exigencies. When a contrary, anti-hegemonic view comes out strong, historiographic conventions, having become habit or mindsets, are all set to transform the contrary view and absorb into a grand paradigm that ultimately only serves the hegemonic ideology. At the same time, hegemonic institutions are automatically set up to not validate, not give authority to contrary views. After all, what is considered truth is what comes from the horse's mouth, and who decides who this privileged horse, the *subject who knows* the truth is?"[21]

One example of this phenomenon is the interesting strategy devised by the defenders of the invasion theory to beat back criticism. They say: The critics are mainly Hindu nationalists motivated by political considerations.

This is nonsense. The invasion/migration theory has been criticized by scholars from all parts of the world, working in different fields of Indic studies. Edmund Leach was not a Hindu nationalist. Neither are Jim Shaffer and Diane Lichtenstein, perhaps the foremost modern scholars of Indian prehistory, who write in a recent essay:[22]

> The South Asian archaeological record reviewed here does not support ... any version of the migration/invasion hypothesis. Rather, the physical distribution of sites and artifacts, stratigraphic data, radiometric dates, and geological data can account from the Vedic oral tradition describing an internal cultural discontinuity of indigenous population movement.

Shaffer and Lichtenstein go to the heart of the matter when they further say about the invasion/migration theories: "*These theories* are significantly diminished by European ethnocentrism, colonialism, racism, and antisemitism. Surely, as South Asian studies enter the twenty-first century, it is time to describe emerging data objectively rather than perpetuate interpretations without regard to the data archaeologists have worked so hard to reveal."[23]

Another archaeologist, Mark Kenoyer, has this to say in his recent book *Ancient Cities of the Indus Valley Civilization* (1998):[24]

> There is no archaeological or biological evidence for invasions or mass migrations into the Indus Valley between the end of the Harappan phase, about 1900 BC and the beginning of the Early Historical period around 600 BC.

Michel Danino expresses thus the lesson of the recent research:[25]

> The central point is the unbroken thread of Indian civilization and culture from pre-Harappan days to the Indus-Sarasvati civilization and the Ganga civilization after the drying of the Sarasvati. Whatever twists and turns Indian civilization may have followed, whatever migrations may have taken place to and from India, nothing in Indian tradition or in archaeology justifies a rigid break between pre-and post-Vedic India; nothing warrants the fallacy of a sharp demarcation between Aryan and Dravidian people, languages, civilizations, even deities ... The neat little labels our Westernized mind has stuck on it after cutting it into well-defined bits—Vedism, Brahminism, Hinduism, and so forth—strain to create separations where non exist. The river flowing down the mountains, then through forests, and finally meandering thought the plains is one and the same.

Those within the hegemonic circle are rendered blind to facts that are inconvenient. It is not so easy to change the minds of people for whom their system is like a religion. But we are in the midst of a paradigmatic change in the understanding of India. The accumulation of evidence has reached a point where it is impossible to ignore it and open-minded people are insisting on a change in the discourse. The politics of this issue has been well presented by the Cambridge archaeologist Dilip Chakrabarti in his important book *Colonial Indology—Sociopolitics of the Ancient Indian Past* (Munshiram Manoharlal, New Delhi, 1997) where many assumptions at the basis of academic Indology have been shown to be wrong.

A Question of Method

Let's for a moment forget the sorry history of the construction of India's past; Edmund Leach has covered that ground very well in his essay. I am prepared to concede that what Leach called racism in Indic studies may not be obvious to the protagonists. Wearing the blinkers of the tradition in their subspeciality, they may believe that they are merely following in the footsteps of their predecessors.

But if a method is wrong the incremental "advances" in the framework will only lead one more astray. There are many examples of this such as the research during the Lysenko regime in the Soviet Union or the work done by the believers in cold fusion.

The basic error in the Orientalist enterprise of Indian prehistory is the *logic* of apportionment of credit for culture to one *race* or another. It is comparable to the search for Aryan and Jewish components in modern science, the absurdity of which is clear to everyone excepting extremist racist groups.

Yet it has become common in Indic studies to write whole volumes on the discovery of the *Aryan* and *Dravidian* components of Indian culture! Words and cultural ideas that have evolved over all of India are now being examined to find which elements of these are Aryan and Dravidian! These are questions to which no definitive answers can be found. If nothing else, this is a colossal waste of academic resources.

There are studies, for example, which trace the caste system to the Indo-European tripartite scheme, and there are still others that trace it to the Dravidian social organization! The Puranas are seen by some to be an organic outgrowth of the Vedic system, and by others to be an expression of the earlier Dravidian Hinduism. This and that of the cultural life are assigned to Aryans and Dravidians with no consistent logic. This list goes on and on.

Edmund Leach ridiculed the method used by Indo-Europeanists. He commended a paper, "Did the Dravidians of India obtain their culture from Aryan immigrant?", written by P.T. Srinivas Iyengar[26] in 1914 (*Anthropos,* vol. 9, pp. 1-15) that clearly shows the propositions of the invasionist/migrationists are "either fictitious or unproved." Iyengar has some fun in the process: "It was reserved for the philologists of the first half of the 19th century to discover that Arya and Dasyu were names of different races. They diligently searched the Veda for indication of this, and their discoveries remind us of the proverbial mouse begotten of the mountain." The philological edifice has been punctured by Swaminathan Aiyar[27] in his remarkable *Dravidian Theories* which appeared in 1975.

Discourse as Theatre

Geertz's eloquent argument, in 1980, for a 'theatre state' interpretation of the Balinese kingdom provides us with a useful insight for the examination of the Indian prehistory paradigm. In a discipline as a theatre, the continuing 'elaborations' of the basic schema are part of a ritual that has nothing to do with the reality of the evidence. Geertz seems to be addressing us when he says, "The state *is a* metaphysical theatre: theatre designed to express a view of the ultimate nature of reality and, at the same time, to shape the existing conditions of life to be consistent with that reality: that is, theatre to present an ontology of the world and, by presenting it, to make it happen—make it actual."[28]

The theatre of Indian prehistory has likewise moulded the current conditions to conform to its reality. It is not physical force but words and ideas that bind people to their academic community.

In the hour of defeat, the theatre state expired with the puputans, the royal parade, with parasols and all, into the fire of the attacking Dutch troops. Is such mass suicide the only end possible for a theatre state? Can there be a peaceful resolution?

The Spread of Humans

Advances in genetics have made it possible to trace ancient migrations. It is now generally accepted that modern man arose in Africa about 200,000 years ago and from there spread first into India and Southeast Asia by coastal migration that probably included some boat crossings. There are several estimates of the time when this spread into India took place. According to geneticists, settlements in India appear about 90,000 years ago. From India there were later northeastern and northwestern migrations into Eurasia and the Far East.

The "Out of Africa theory" has superseded the earlier multiregional model according to which the Europeans, the Asians, and Indonesians arose independently in different parts of the world. There is overwhelming evidence that archaic lines—such as Neanderthals in Europe—simply died out, and the specific characteristics of the different races is not a consequence of a mixing of the regional and modern populations but rather of adaptation to unique climatic conditions.

Microevolution, as in the mutations of the mitochondrial DNA (inherited from the mother) and the Y chromosome (inherited from the father), helps us trace and connect populations across time and region. When the random mutations are calibrated one has a genetic clock. The clock can be validated in a variety of ways; for example, by using the knowledge of when the potato plant spread around the world from its Andean origin.

Even without historical evidence related to the spread of the potato plant, a scientist can deduce the Andean origin of the plant from the fact that there exist many varieties of it in Peru and just a few lines in Asia, Europe, and Africa. Given the genetic clock and the distance between the DNA of the European and the current Peruvian varieties, one can estimate the period the plant was taken to Europe.

The new findings turn on its head the previous view of the origin of Indians. The earlier view, popular in Indian history books, was that the Indian population came in two waves from the northwest around four or five thousand years ago, displacing the earlier aboriginals, descendents of regional archaic groups.

The new view is that subsequent to the rise of modern mankind in Africa, it found a second home in India, which is the point of migration for the populations of Europe, North Africa, China and Japan. The migrants in India slowly adapted to the wide climatic conditions in the sub-continent (from the tropical to the extreme cold of the Himalayan region) leading to the rise of the Caucasoid and the Mongoloid races.

A recent paper in the journal *Science* reporting on the analysis of the DNA of the Orang Asli, the original inhabitants of Malaysia, confirms this view. According to it a single migration out of Africa took the southern route to India, Southeast Asia and Australasia. At this time Europe was too cold for human habitation. About 50,000 years ago, when deserts turned into grasslands, an out of India migration populated the Near East and Europe, another migration went northeast through China and over the now submerged Bering Strait into the Americas. This agrees with the earliest known modern human sites of the Near East (45,000 years ago) and Europe (40,000 years ago).

It is likely that the earliest sites on the coastline that were occupied by the first migrants are now under water, since sea level has risen more than 60 metres since the last Ice Age. This widespread inundation is likely to be the basis of the flood myths that are common to all ancient cultures.

This view not only changes our understanding of the peopling of India, but also of Southeast Asia. For some time the academic view was that the Polynesians and the Indonesians were latecomers into their lands from China. The new view is that the habitation of the Southeast Asia is almost as old as that of India and Australia, and the Chinese, as also the Japanese, are relative latecomers into northeast Asia.

Dental anthropology provides important clues in the retracing of ancient migrations. The Indian type of teeth is called *Sundadont*, and it is also found amongst Southeast Asians, Micronesians, and Polynesians. Contrasted from Sundadonty is *Sinodonty* (dental features that include shovel-shaped incisors, single-rooted upper first premolars, triple rooted lower first molars and other attributes), the degree of which is seen to increase as one travels north through the Mongoloid populations of mainland East Asia, and it is seen in extreme in the Americas. The South Asian origin of the pure-blood Ainu inhabitants of Japan is confirmed from their Sundadonty.

The Kennewick Man

The Kennewich Man, a 9,300 year old skeleton was discovered in 1996 on the banks of the Columbia River near the Washington town of Kennewick. The skeleton was caught in a controversy because the Native American groups did not wish the body of an ancestor to be dishonored. On the other hand, there was much interest to study the skeleton further because its features were very different from that of the typical north Asian type from which the Native Americans are descended.

Scientific study has shown that the Kennewick Man represents the *Indian (South Asian) type*. The skull is long and narrow and the teeth are of the Sundadont type. This should not be extrapolated to mean that the Kennewick man actually came from the Indian subcontinent. But it confirms the spread of the Indian type all over the ancient world, from which it was displaced by later adaptations to different climates.

The Spread of Languages

When the theory of the Aryan invasions into India is replaced by an "Out of India" viewpoint, one can readily explain regularities in languages that are spread widely. Linguists see connections between India and languages that extend to distant lands. Thus the Indo-Pacific family covers the languages of the Australian aborigines and the Papuans, the Austro-Asiatic cuts across from India to the Pacific (the Munda in India, the Thai, and the Vietnamese), and the Dravidian has connections with the Altaic (Japanese, Korean, and the Turkic).

Within India, the connections between the structure and vocabulary of the north and the south Indian languages indicate much internal migration of people. The genetic evidence indicates that the Dravidian languages are the more ancient, and the Aryan languages *evolved in India* over thousands of years before migrants carried them westward to Europe. The proto-Dravidian languages reached northeast Asia through the sea route. If Aryan evolved out of proto-Dravidian, the attempt of the linguists to construct a *pure* proto-Dravidian vocabulary is in all probability wrong.

The idea that the development of the Aryan languages took place in India explains how a variety of such languages are to be found in the sub-continent. Both the so-called *kentum* and *satem* language families are represented: Bangani is *kentum*, it is found in the Himalayan region; and languages such as Sanskrit, Hindi, and Assamese are *satem*.

Let us return to Edmund Leach, who was a good anthropologist and a sober man. He was for many years a professor at Cambridge and, later, a provost at King's College. He used the charge of racism against Indo-Europeanists deliberately. Ending his essay, he said, "[To] bring about a shift in this entrenched paradigm is like trying to cut down a 300-year-old oak tree with a penknife. But the job will have to be done one day."

Academic study on ancient India will remain "like a patient etherized upon a table" unless it finds a proper center and fresh energy. This center will be located only as a result of critiques like that of Leach. But what about energy? Will it be provided by the financial support of Indians in the West, who have made enormous fortunes in the knowledge and computer industry? I don't think so, at least not in the near future. The racism at the basis of Indic studies, which Indians have experienced in their own education and of which they continue to hear from their children in college, has made them reluctant to support academic programs.

The Aryan affair is, nevertheless, of great interest to the anthropologist. Paraphrasing Leach, one may raise questions like: Why do serious people spend their lives in the elaboration of a wrong theory? It seems to be like the scholiasts of the Middle Ages spinning volumes on how many angels can rest on the point of a needle!

5

India and Europe

It is common to speak of civilizational ideas, but do they exist? For example, are the *doshas* of Ayurveda peculiarly Indian since they are a tripartite classification that is basic to the Vedic system of knowledge? Plato introduced a similar system based on three humors into Greek medicine, with a central role to the idea of breath *(pneuma* in Greek). But this centrality of breath *(prana* in Sanskrit) is already a feature of the much older Vedic thought. So do we agree with the theory that Plato borrowed the elements of the wind, the gall, and the phlegm, from the earlier tridosha theory, and that the transmission occurred via the Persian empire? Others claim that any similarities between the Indian and the Greek medical systems must be a result of the shared Indo-European heritage and what may appear to be Indian is actually Indo-European, to be assigned an age before the dispersal of the Indians and the Europeans from their original homeland.

Indian and European traditions appear to have three hierarchical functions: sacred sovereignty, force, and fecundity, represented by the categories of *brahman, rajan* (or *kshatra*), and *vish*. Religious and political sovereignty is conceived as a dual category: the magician-king and the jurist-priest. In India, this duality is in the roles of the *rajan* and *brahman*; in Rome, of *rex* and *flamen*.

The magician-king (Varuna in India or Romulus in Rome) initiates in violence the social order that the jurist-priest (Mitra in India or Numa in Rome) develops in peace. Magical sovereignty operates by means of bonds and debts, whereas juridical sovereignty employs pacts and faith.

There is similarity between the Indian and the Greek religions as also in the society sketched in the Mahabharata and Homeric poems. Metempsychosis is known in both places. The imagery of the *world-egg*, so central to Vedic thought, is described in the Orphic legends.

These parallels are the result either of shared origins, migration, or cultural diffusion, or a combination of the three. In themselves, they cannot help us in determining the history of the system, but the articulation of the basic scheme has distinct characteristics in different regions. It is this articulation—this style—that represents a civilizational idea. Perhaps the clearest representation of this is in the styles of art, painting, music, and literature.

As an illustration of a civilizational idea, consider the notion of self in the upanishadic dialogues, which the texts assert is the essence of the Veda, its secret knowledge. A similar emphasis on self-knowledge is introduced into Greek thought by the Pythagoreans and the Orphics. Corresponding to the three gunas of *sattva, rajas, tamas,* Plato spoke of three categories *logistikon, thumos, epithumia* and he used a three-part classification for society. The amplification of the ideas of self and society occurred in different ways in the two civilizations. The commonality of purpose between Vedantic ideas and the philosophy of Plato is not as crucial as the manner of the exposition that has distinct flavors which may be called Indian and Greek. But one may ask if it is possible to go back before the time of the Greek philosophers and see the evidence of intrusive ideas before they were assimilated.

The intrusion of Indic people—and, concomitantly, their ideas—in the Near East is well known. An Indic element was a part of the Mitanni who, by the 15th century BC, had expanded their power from the shores of the Mediterranean to the Zagros mountains. In a treaty with the Hittites, the Mitanni king swears by the Indic gods Mitra, Varuna, Indra, and Nasatya. Other Mitanni documents, uncovered in the archives at Bogazkoy (Hittite) and El Amarna (Egypt) clearly point to Indic influences. A Hittite text on horse-training and chariotry uses Sanskrit numerals; a Hurrian text uses Sanskrit words to describe the colour of horses. The Kassites, who ruled Mesopotamia for several centuries in the second millennium BC, had an Indic element, representing, here as elsewhere in the region, a ruling aristocracy.

This Indic element is likely to have played a role in the development of the cultural and religious complexes of Egypt and the Near East in the second millennium BC. The beginnings of this particular intrusion are seen around 1800 BC. Around 1650, an Indic people occupied the Nile delta for about 100 years; these people are described as the Hyksos, the Foreign Princes. Egypt's new eschatological visions and innovations in myth are taken as the evidence for this presence, which flows in logical sequence to their presence in West Asia. A still earlier intrusion of Eastern ideas into Egypt has also been assumed based on the readings of Pyramid Texts of about 2600 BC. The military activity of the Hittite king Hattusilis is taken as the vehicle for this process. But that early period does not concern us here. A memory of the supremacy of the Indic (or Indo-Iranian) region in religious and, concomitantly, artistic ideas is preserved in an ancient

Pahlavi text. The world is divided into three regions: the west (Rome) with riches; the north and east (Turkestan and the deserts) with martial turbulence; the south (Iran and India) with religion, law, and supreme royalty.

Could the Near East have served as a conduit for Indic ideas to Europe? To answer this we trace the passage of certain Indic ideas in art and astronomy to the Graeco-Roman world.

The language of myth often represents astronomical and spiritual knowledge. There exist structural similarities in many myths of the ancient world and these myths may be read as a narrative on the shifting frame of time due to precession. Myths are also a description of the ongoing transformations in the mind's sky. This dual meaning can provide us specific imagery making it possible to trace its history.

Consider Venus, the planet and the Roman goddess of natural productivity and also of love and beauty. The Greeks called this planet Aphrodite and also Eosphoros or the bringer of light when it appeared as a morning star, and Hesperos when it appeared as the evening star. It is believed that the Greeks first did not know that the two stars were the same but by the time of the Pythagoreans this identity was known. The Roman Venus derived her characteristics from the Greek Aphrodite who in turn appears to have been based on the Babylonian Ishtar. In Greek legend Aphrodite was born in Kupris or Cyprus; Kupris, a feminine deity, was derived from the masculine Kupros. In India, there is the Rigvedic attestation (10.123) of Vena as the name for this planet. Later texts use Shukra as another name. So we have have linguistic affinity in these names: Venus and Vena, Kupros and Shukra.

The Rigveda describes two aspects of Venus: one, as Gandharva who is the patron of singing and the arts; and the other, who is the son of the sun and an asura. These conceptions, together with the meaning of Vena as longing and love, lead to both the later mythologies to be found in India as well as in west Asia.

It has been suggested that the representation of the goddess in Mesopotamia and later on in Greece was under the influence of Indian ideas. Perhaps the evidence of the first conceptualizations of the goddess can help us with the chronology of the ideas in India. Aphrodite, like Lakshmi, is born out of the sea. But the Indian story is technically more sound because here the birth is out of churning, like that of butter out of milk, whereas the circumstances of Aphrodite's birth are not described. Also, Ishtar couldn't have been prior to Vena because it has only one of the many elements to be found in the Rigvedic hymn 10.123.

Vena knows the secret of immortality; this presumably has reference to the fact that Venus emerges again after being obscured by the sun. In the Puranic glosses of this story Shukra is swallowed up by Shiva and later on expelled as semen; this is a play on the etymology of Shukra as bright. The Puranas tell us how the gods learnt the secret of immortality from Shukra by subterfuge. There is another remembrance of the immortality of Venus in the myth of Phoenix, a word cognate with Vena. Phoenix rises again after death, warmed by the rays of the sun. The Indian sources, namely the Rigveda and the Puranas, explain the whole basis of the Vena-Shukra myth at several levels. In Mesopotamia and in Greece and Rome, only scattered meanings are encountered which lead us to the conclusion that these ideas traveled from India to Europe by way of Mesopotamia.

Scholars of comparative mythology have pointed out other parallels. Scholars have compared episodes from the epics and the Puranas with the myths of various European people and found crucial similarity in detail. While some invoke the tripartite underpinnings of the Indo-European thought to explain this similarity, it is more likely that there was some transmission of stories like the ones that occurred in the later transmission of Indian fables and Jatakas. The Indian stories are according to a self-conscious logic so the encyclopaedic authors of the Puranas had no trouble churning them out in large numbers. There is a deep and comprehensive exposition of the myths in the Indian texts. The European stories, in contrast, are disconnected. The Rigveda contains a decisively greater portion of the common Indo-European mythological heritage.[29] In fact there is hardly a major motif common in two or more of the other branches that is not found in the Rigveda. This is even more true if the Puranic literature is considered.

Art

Given the above evidence, it is not surprising that the themes and motifs of the rock art and the later Harappan seals are repeated in the Near East and in Greece. One of these is the image of the hero—the Gilgamesh figure—that is found both in the rock art and in the Harappan seals. This appears to validate the idea of interaction between India and its western regions in early centuries of the third millennium BC.

We now look at a few specific forms and symbols from Western art for their Indian parallels.

Heroes, Sacrifice

Although the Kirttimukha, a guardian of the threshold, is dated somewhat late in Indian art, its basis is squarely within the Indian mythological tradition. Many scholars have argued that the image of the Gorgon must be viewed as an intrusive

Indic idea or a Greek interpretation of the Kirttimukha assimilated atop a different legend. The forehead markings of the Gorgon and the single-eye of the cyclops are seen as Indian elements. This may have been a byproduct of the interaction with the Indian foot soldiers who fought for the armies of the Persian and the Medean empires. But there were also Indian traders in Greece, just as there were Greek trading settlements in India. This is supported by the fact that the name of the Mycenaean Greek city Tiryns—the place where the most ancient monuments of Greece are to be found—is the same as that of the most powerful Indian sea-faring people called the Tirayans.

The Perseus-Gorgon story is replete with Indian elements, especially the connection of the myth with Lycia. According to the art historian David Napier, "This ancient kingdom figures predominantly in Greek mythology as the location of the exotic: a place of ivory, peacocks, and 'many-eyed' cows; a place to which Greeks went to marry and assimilate that which to the pre-classical mind represented everything exotic ... In the British Museum we find a Lycian building, the roof of which is clearly the descendant of an ancient South Asian style. Proof of this hypothesis comes not only in what may appear to be a superficial similarity, nor in the many 'Asian' references with which Lycia is associated, but in the very name of the structure which dates to the mid-fourth century BC. For this is the so-called 'Tomb of the Payava' a Graeco-Indian Pallava if there was one. And who were the Tirayans, but the ancestors of two of the most famous of ancient Indian clans, the Pallavas and Cholas?"[30]

Funerary Art

Indian mythology has rich descriptions of Indra's city, the paradise, with its water nymphs and gardens. Octavio Alvarez suggests[31] that these Vedic themes of afterlife are sketched on Etruscan tombs. He traces the transmission of these themes via Egypt, where the souls were no longer received by the tragic death-god Osiris, but by the enchanting Hathor, the goddess of joy and love. Likewise, in the earlier Graeco-Roman conception of the afterworld the souls were supposed to exist *without midriff*, i.e., deprived of food and sex. But ultimately the ideas of the Vedic heaven, where in the city of Indra are all pleasures and eternal youth, displaced these older views, and Alvarez is able to explain the new symbols of resurrection used in the Etruscan and later funerary art. He establishes a connection between the water-nymphs in the Graeco-Roman mythology and the apsarases of the Vedic mythology.

We note that this western interpretation of Vedic afterlife was a literal rendering of a metaphor. The Vedic paradise transcends space and time and it represents an absorption into Brahman. The idea of paradise as a pleasure garden was later adopted by Islam.

Alvarez is able to explain the iconography of the Etruscan sea-sarcophagi very convincingly using Indian parallels. He describes eight basic elements:

1. The scene is the celestial ocean, abode of the departed souls, quite like Indra's paradise.

2. The females are the apsarases, water-nymphs. On early sarcophagi and sepulchral imagery they wear the Indian hairdo and earrings, but are otherwise nude, conforming to the Indian models. They are shown with prominent bellies and heavy backsides intentionally framed by drapes in the Indian manner.

3. The babies are the souls of the departed who reappear in paradise. This reappearance is connected to the idea of rebirth.

4. The flowers are the immediate vehicles of rebirth according to the idea of the birth out of Lotus.

5. The breast-feeding of the soul-babies shows the reception and nourishment by the heavenly hosts.

6. The sea-centauri are gandharvas. As the male counterparts and lovers of the apsarases, they show fins and fish-tails to set them apart from the Graeco-Roman centauri.

7. The amorini who fill the atmosphere are the Mediterranean symbols to denote the celestial ocean, which is so glowingly described in India's eschatology.

8. The portrait of the deceased was shown within a sea-shell, no doubt to indicate the rebirth in the Celestial Ocean.

There are other Indian elements in the iconography, such as garlands and the betel nut.

The Gundestrup Cauldron

Consider the case of the Gundestrup cauldron, found in Denmark a hundred years ago. This silver bowl has been dated to around the middle of the 2nd century BC. The sides are decorated with various scenes of war and sacrifice: deities wrestling beasts, a goddess flanked by elephants, a meditating figure wearing stag's antlers. That the iconography must be Indic is suggested by the elephant (totally out of context in Europe) with the goddess and the yogic figure. According to the art historian Timothy Taylor, "A shared pictorial and technical tradition stretched from India to Thrace, where the cauldron was made, and thence to Denmark. Yogic rituals, for example, can be inferred from the poses of an antler-bearing man on the cauldron and of an ox-headed figure on a seal impress from the Indian city of Mohenjo-Daro … Three other Indian links: ritual baths of goddesses with elephants (the Indian goddess is Lakshmi); wheel gods (the Indian is Vishnu); the goddesses with braided hair and paired birds (the Indian is Hariti)."[32] Taylor speculates that members of an Indian itinerant artisan class, not unlike the later Gypsies in Europe who also originate in India, must have been the creators of the cauldron.

Egyptian Terracottas

Many terracottas excavated by Petrie at Memphis in Egypt were declared by him to be Indian. These figures date from the Graeco-Roman period and it is accepted that an Indian colony existed in Memphis from about the 5th century BC onwards. Reviewing the evidence, the scholar Harle concludes that the figures were made by these Indian colonists. Harle points to the pose, which in two cases is lalitasana and rajalilasana. He suggest that the plastic feeling, however hard to define, is also Indian. There are other features as well which recall certain Indian figures: the corpulence, a dhoti-like lower garment and, in one case, an armlet on the right arm and a scarf over the left shoulder. These features point to an Indian Panchika (Kubera) from Gandhara of the early Panchika and Hariti sculpture in the Peshawar Museum. The figures include one that has traditionally been taken to be Harpocrates, the son of Isis and Osiris. But it is possible that for the Indian colonists the figure represented Krishna-Vasudeva as the child-god. Two bronzes of this child-god have been found in Begram and Taxila.

The Roma and the Persistence of Memory

Historians tell us that we represent the fourth wave of major migration from post-Harappan India to the West. The first happened about 2000 BC as a result of the dislocations caused in north India by earthquakes that altered the direction of major rivers and caused the drying up of the Sarasvati valleys. It is soon after this time that the Indic element begins to all over West Asia and Europe. Some

Druze and Kurds claim that they are descendents of Indians from this period, but this belief could be a modern myth.

Herodotus in his *Histories* speaks of the contingents of Indian soldiers in the Persian armies that battled the Greeks 1,500 years later. Indian colonies were situated in Babylon, Alexandria, Memphis, and Rome. But this, as the previous migration, is remembered only by historians. This second wave extended over centuries. For example, Firdausi, the author of *Shahnamah*, tells us that during his reign, the Persian king Behram Gaur (5th century AD) asked his father-in-law in India to send him 10,000 musicians. What influence this massive migration had on the music of Eurasia, we will never be able to estimate.

The third wave is remembered with greater clarity. This was the Roma, or Gypsies, who left India a thousand years ago as a result of the Arab and Turkish wars. According to the *Chachnama*, a contemporary account of Muhammad bin Qasim's campaigns in Sindh in 712-3, several thousand Jat warriors were captured as prisoners of war and deported to Iraq and elsewhere as slaves. A few hundred thousand women were likewise enslaved. The process of enslavement was accelerated during the campaigns of Mahmud of Ghazni. Abu Nasr Muhammad Utbi, the secretary and chronicler of Mahmud, informs us that 500,000 men and women were captured in Waihind alone in 1001-2. During his seventeen invasions, Mahmud Ghaznavi is estimated to have enslaved more than a million people. According to Utbi, "they were taken to Ghazna, and merchants came from different cities to purchase them, so that the countries of Mawarau-un-Nahr, Iraq and Khurasan were filled with them."

The famed linguist and historian, Ian Hancock, himself of Romani ancestry, has argued that it was to escape this ongoing enslavement in the battlegrounds of Middle India, that many soldiers, together with their families, migrated west. Some say they were mainly Rajputs, but perhaps they did not constitute a single group, rather representing a wide spectrum of Indians society. These migrating families became the ancestors to the Roma. So their experience is the experience of a part of India that was separated from it a thousand years ago.

Passing through various lands, the Roma started appearing in Europe in the Middle Ages. But very soon they discovered a horrible welcome: that of removal by expulsion, repression, assimilation and, later, extermination. Here are a few randomly chosen accounts in various European countries:

The King of Denmark, in 1589, decreed that any leader of a Roma band found on Danish soil was to be sentenced to death. In the seventeenth century, any vessel bringing in Roma would be confiscated. From that time on, and until 1849, any Rom found in Denmark was subject to deportation. Gypsy hunts were organized with rewards to those who captured a Rom. Sweden also enacted harsh laws to deter the Roma. They were not allowed to enter the country. Those who managed to do so were immediately expelled. Those who failed to leave were brutally attacked or hanged. This forced many Roma to go into hiding and marginalized them from society, or forced them to assimilate.

France enacted a series of expulsion laws beginning in 1510. Throughout the sixteenth century any Roma caught in the country were flogged. In the following century, Romani women who were captured had their heads shaved and were sent to workhouses. The men were put into chains in galleys.

In the sixteenth century England, Roma were ordered to leave or be imprisoned because the English believed them to be sorcerers, thieves and cheats. Signs were posted in the English countryside, telling the Roma that they must leave England. Those who remained were given forty days to leave. Failure to do so meant death. If they were lucky, they were deported to their colonies as cheap sources of labor. In most countries, the speaking of Romani was forbidden.

Switzerland allowed Gypsy hunts in the sixteenth century, as did Holland in the eighteenth century. In the former Moravia, it was within law to cut off the left ear of all Romani women who were caught. In Bohemia, removal of the right ear was legal.

In the Romanian principalities of Moldavia and Wallachia the Roma were enslaved in the fifteenth century. Once freed, a number of restrictive measures were taken against them, including a 1740 law that stated that no Rom could perform metalworking outside his tent. This law was aimed at any attempt by the Roma to compete against native metalworkers.

The fundamental hostility towards the Roma remained unchanged, reaching its most tragic limits in Hitler's Germany before and during World War II. The Roma were seen as asocial, a source of crime and culturally inferior. When Adolf Hitler came to power in Germany in 1933, his Nazi administration inherited anti-Gypsy laws that had been in force since the Middle Ages.

On 15 September 1935, Jews were restricted by the Nuremberg Law for the Protection of Blood and Honor, and Roma were added later in 1937. This law forbade intermarriage or sexual intercourse with the perceived foreign peoples. Criteria for classification as a Rom were twice as strict as those applied to Jews. If two of a person's eight great-grandparents were even part-Rom, that person "had too much Gypsy blood to be allowed to live."

In 1937, the Nazi-occupied countries began to force the Roma into concentration camps. Many of them were worked to death as slave laborers in the camp quarry or at outlying arms factories. At first, there were no gas chambers but thousands were shot, hanged, or tortured to death by the camp's guards. Other prisoners were sterilized to prevent them from having children of their own.

A few years later a program of liquidation began. Roma were beaten and clubbed to death, herded into the gas chambers, and forced to dig their own graves. The fate of the Roma paralleled the tragic fate of the Jews, who were also imprisoned and exterminated. They were tortured, used for inhuman scientific experiments, and put to death in the infamous gas chambers.

It is estimated that over a million Roma were murdered from 1935 to the end of World War II. After the war, the Roma received little, if any, reparations from any government for their losses and suffering. Not a single Rom was called to testify at the Nuremberg Trials, or has been to any of the subsequent war crime tribunals. Until the 1970s, many Nazi-era laws remained on the books. In 1982, the German government was one of the first (and few) to belatedly recognize the atrocities committed against Romani people during World War II.

The Roma have survived in the most difficult situation and for this they deserve to be saluted by all. They have also given a lot to Europe—music, dance, arts and crafts, and shown an indomitable will to survive.

6

Vedic Knowledge and Astronomy

Having surveyed the connections of India with its Western neighbors, we return to the question of the nature of the Vedic system of knowledge. Astronomy provides us important clues here. It also provides us means to decode references of chronological significance in the Vedas.

Due to precession of the earth, the seasons shift at a rate of about a month every two thousand years. Some Vedic notices mark the beginning of the year and that of the vernal equinox in Orion; this was the case around 4500 BC. There are other astronomical references from the subsequent millennia. This indicates a long period of time over which astronomy developed into a science.

Fire altars, with astronomical basis, have been found in the third millennium cities of India. The texts that describe their designs are conservatively dated to the first millennium BC, but their contents appear to be much older. Basing his analysis on the Pythagorean triples in Greece, Babylon, and India, the historian of science A. Seidenberg concluded that the knowledge contained in these texts—the Shulba Sutras—goes back to at least 1700 BC. More recent archaeological evidence, together with the astronomical references in the texts, suggests that this knowledge belongs to the third millennium BC.

The Vedanga Jyotisha (VJ), the text that describes some of the astronomical knowledge of the times of altar ritual, has an internal date of c. 1350 BC, obtained from its assertion that the winter solstice was at the asterism Shravishtha (Delphini). Recent archaeological discoveries support such an early date, and so this book assumes great importance in the understanding of the earliest astronomy.

Vedic ritual was based on the times for the full and the new moons, solstices and the equinoxes. The year was known to be somewhat more than 365 days and a bit less than 366 days. The solar year was marked variously in the many different astronomical traditions that marked the Vedic world. In one tradition, an extra eleven days were added to the lunar year of 354 days. According to one text,

41

five more days are required over the nominal year of 360 days to complete the seasons, since four days are too short and six days are too long.

Veda means knowledge in Sanskrit. The early Vedic times were characterized by the composition of hymns that were collected together in four books. The oldest of these books is the Rigveda; the one that deals with the performance of ritual is called Yajurveda.

The central idea behind the Vedic system is the notion of *bandhu*, connections, between the astronomical, the terrestrial, and the physiological. These connections were described in terms of number or other characteristics. An example is the 360 bones of the infant (which later fuse into the 206 bones of the adult) and the 360 days of the year. Although the Vedic books speak often about astronomical phenomena, it is only recently that the astronomical substratum of the Vedas has been examined. One can see a plausible basis behind the equivalences. Research has shown that all life comes with its inner clocks. Living organisms have rhythms that are matched to the periods of the sun or the moon. There are quite precise biological clocks of 24-hour (according to the day), 24 hour 50 minutes (according to the lunar day since the moon rises roughly 50 minutes later every day) or its half representing the tides, 29.5 days (the period from one new moon to the next), and the year. Monthly rhythms, averaging 29.5 days, are reflected in the reproductive cycles of many marine plants and those of animals. The menstrual period is a synodic month and the average duration of pregnancy is nine synodic months. There are other biological periodicities of longer durations.

The astronomy of the Indian fire altars of the Vedic times shows that this knowledge was also coded in the organization of the Rigveda, which was taken to be a symbolic altar of hymns. This is described at length in my book *The Astronomical Code of the Rgveda*. The examination of the Rigveda is of unique significance since this ancient book has been preserved with incredible fidelity. This fidelity was achieved by remembering the text not only as a sequence of syllables (and words) but also through several different permutations of these syllables.

That the number of syllables and the verses of the Rigveda are according to an astronomical plan is claimed in other books of nearly the same antiquity such as the Shatapatha Brahmana. The Rigveda may be considered an ancient word monument. It appears that the tradition, insisting that not a single syllable of the Rigveda be altered, arose from an attempt to be true to observed astronomical facts.

Vedic ritual was generally performed at an altar. The altar design was based on astronomical numbers related to the reconciliation of the lunar and solar years.

Vedic rites were meant to mark the passage of time. A considerable part of the ritual deals with altar construction. The fire altars symbolized the universe and there were three types of altars representing the earth, the space and the sky. The altar for the earth was drawn as circular whereas the sky (or heaven) altar was drawn as square. The geometric problems of circulature of a square and that of squaring a circle are a result of equating the earth and the sky altars. As we know these problems are among the earliest considered in ancient geometry.

The fire altars were surrounded by 360 enclosing stones. Of these, 21 were around the earth altar, 78 around the space altar and 261 around the sky altar. In other words, the earth, the space, and the sky are symbolically assigned the numbers 21, 78, and 261. Considering the earth/cosmos dichotomy, the two numbers are 21 and 339 since cosmos includes the space and the sky.

The main altar was built in five layers. The basic square shape was modified to several forms, such as falcon and turtle. These altars were built in five layers, of a thousand bricks of specified shapes. The construction of these altars required the solution to several geometric and algebraic problems.

The main altar was an area that was taken to be equivalent to the nominal year of 360 days. Now, each subsequent year, the shape was to be reproduced with the area increased by one unit.

The ancient Indians spoke of two years: (1) lunar, which is a fraction more than 354 days (360 tithis); and (2) solar, which is in excess of 365 days (between 371 and 372 tithis). A well-known altar ritual says that altars should be constructed in a sequence of 95, with progressively increasing areas. The increase in the area, by one unit yearly, in building progressively larger fire altars is 48 tithis which is about equal to the intercalation required to make the lunar year in tithis equal to the solar year in tithis. But there is a residual excess which in 95 years adds up to 89 tithis; it appears that after this period such a correction was made. The 95 year cycle corresponds to the tropical year being equal to 365.24675 days. The cycles needed to harmonize various motions led to the concept of increasing periods and world ages.

The number of syllables in the Rigveda confirms the textual references that the book was to represent a symbolic altar. According to various early texts, the number of syllables in the Rigveda is 432,000, which is the number of muhurtas (1 day = 30 muhurtas) in forty years. In reality the syllable count is somewhat less because certain syllables are supposed to be left unspoken.

The verse count of the Rigveda can be viewed as the number of *sky* days in forty years or 261 x 40 = 10,440, and the verse count of all the Vedas is 261 x 78 = 20,358.

The Rigveda is divided into ten books with a total of 1,017 hymns which are placed into 216 groups. Are these numbers accidental or is there a deliberate plan behind the choice? One would expect that if the Rigveda is considered akin to the five-layered altar described in the Brahmanas then the first two books should correspond to the space intermediate to the earth and the sky. Now the number that represents space is 78. When used with the multiplier of 3 for the three worlds, this yields a total of 234 hymns which is indeed the number of hymns in these two books. One may represent the Rigvedic books as a five-layered altar of books (with two books in each layer) as shown below:

Table: Hymns in the altar of books

191	114
104	92
87	75
62	58
43	191

The choice of this arrangement must have been prompted by the considerable regularity in the hymn counts. Thus the hymn count separations diagonally across the two columns are 29 each for Book 4 to Book 5 and Book 6 to Book 7 and they are 17 each for the second column for Book 4 to Book 6 and Book 6 to Book 8. Books 5 and 7 in the first column are also separated by 17; Books 5 and 7 also add up to the total for either Book 1 or Book 10. Another regularity is that the middle three layers are indexed by order from left to right whereas the bottom and the top layers are in the opposite sequence.

Furthermore, Books [4+6+8+9] = 339, and these books may be taken to represent the spine of the altar. The underside of the altar now consists of the Books [2+3+5+7] = 296, and the feet and the head Books [1+10] = 382. The numbers 296 and 382 are each 43 removed from the fundamental Rigvedic number of 339.

The texts speak about the altar of chhandas and meters, so we would expect that the total hymn count of 1017 and the group count of 216 have particular significance. Owing to the pervasive tripartite ideology of the Vedic books we choose to view the hymn number as 339 x 3. The tripartite ideology refers to the consideration of time in three divisions of past, present, and future and the consideration of space in the three divisions of the northern celestial hemisphere, the plane that is at right angle to the earth's axis, and the southern celestial hemisphere.

One can argue that another parallel with the representation of the layered altar was at work in the group total of 216. Since the Rigvedic altar of hymns was meant to symbolically take one to the sky, the abode of gods, it appears that the number 216 represents the distance taken to separate the earth from the sky; where 108 is the distance to the sun. The Rigvedic code then expresses a fundamental connection between the numbers 339 and 108.

In the cosmic model used by the ancients, the earth is at the center, and the sun and the moon orbit the earth at different distances with the sun halfway to the sky. If the number 108 was taken to represent symbolically the distance between the earth and the sun, the question arises as to why it was done. The answer is apparent if one considers the actual distances of the sun and the moon. The number 108 is roughly the average distance that the sun is in terms of its own diameter from the earth; likewise, it is also the average distance that the moon is in terms of its own diameter from the earth. It is owing to this marvelous coincidence that the angular size of the sun and the moon, viewed from the earth, is about identical. Most astonishingly, the diameter of the sun is roughly 108 times the diameter of the earth, but it is very unlikely that this equation was a part of the Indian scheme.

It is easy to compute this number. The angular measurement of the sun can be obtained quite easily during an eclipse. The angular measurement of the moon can be made on any clear full moon night. A easy check on this measurement would be to make a person hold a pole at a distance that is exactly 108 times its length and confirm that the angular measurement is the same. Nevertheless, the computation of this number would require careful observations.

The second number 339 is simply the number of disks of the sun or the moon to measure the path across the sky: $\pi \times 108 = 339$.

We return to a further examination of the numbers 296, 339, and 382 in the design of the Rigvedic altar. It has been suggested that 339 has an obvious significance as the number of sun-steps during the average day or the equinox, and the other numbers are likely to have a similar significance. In other words, 296 is the number of sun-steps during the winter solstice and 382 is the number of sun-steps during the summer solstice.

There also exists compelling evidence that the periods of the planets were known and used in the Rigvedic astronomical code.

7

A Distant Looking Glass

The temple in ancient India was more than a congregational place. One went there to socialize, to participate in festivals, to find one's guru, and for knowledge. The temple architecture itself was a mirror of the cosmos. Let me peer into a looking glass—distant in time and space—that best embodies, in brick and stone, the meaning and role of a temple. I am speaking of the great Vishnu temple of Angkor Wat in Kampuchea (Cambodia), one of most impressive and enduring architectural monuments of the world. The plan of this incomparable temple reveals to us many secrets that were lost to India for centuries. These are secrets about the nature of temple design and, ultimately, about the fundamental bases of Indian culture.

Together with my friends, the historian of astronomy Graham Millar of Halifax, Canada, and Lokesh Chandra, India's foremost scholar of Asia, I have investigated the architecture of this temple during the past few years and discovered amazing continuity with Vedic knowledge.[33] But this is not the appropriate place to speak about the technical details of this surprising continuity; here I merely present a broad outline of what we know about this temple.

The Angkor Vishnu temple was built by the Khmer Emperor Suryavarman II, who reigned during AD 1113-50. One of the many temples built from AD 879–1191, it arose when the Khmer civilization was at the height of its power. Although Vishnu is its main deity, the temple, through its sculpture, pays homage to all the Vedic gods and goddesses, including Shiva.

Apart from its other uses as a place for ritual, dance and drama, study and scholarship—it had many libraries—, the temple served as a practical observatory where the rising sun was aligned on the equinox and solstice days with the western entrance of the temple. The temple architecture reflects calendric and cosmological time cycles.

The most impressive aspect of the design of this temple is that the representation of the universe—which is what a temple is supposed to be—occurs in several layers in a recursive fashion, mirroring the Vedic idea that the microcosm symbolizes the macrocosm at many levels of expression. This is done not only in the domain of numbers and directions, but also using appropriate mythological themes, and historical incidents. The mythological scenes skillfully use the oppositions and complementarities between gods, goddesses, asuras, and humans defined over ordinary and sacred time and space.

The temple complex is vast: it is a bit less that a square mile in size. The dimensions of the temple reflect various astronomical numbers. For example, the west-east axis represents the periods of the yugas. In the central tower, the topmost elevation has external axial dimensions of 189.00 cubit east-west, and 176.37 cubit north-south, with the sum of 365.37. This division of the almost exact length of the solar year into unequal halves remained a mystery until it was found to be based on the Vedic numbers for the asymmetric motion of the sun.

The Khmer kings of Kampuchea (Cambodia) trace their ancestry to the legendary Indian Kaundinya and to Soma, a Khmer princess. At first there were several warring kings. The state was unified by King Jayavarman II who, in 802 in a ceremony near Angkor, declared himself a "universal ruler" (*chakravartin*).

The kings of the Khmer empire ruled over a domain that, at its broadest, reached from what is now southern Vietnam to Yunan, China and from Vietnam westward to the Bay of Bengal. The structures one sees at Angkor today, more than 100 temples in all, are the surviving religious remains of a grand social and administrative metropolis whose other buildings—palaces, public buildings, and houses—were built of wood and are long since decayed and gone. As in most parts of India where wood was plentiful, only the gods had the right to live in houses of stone or brick; the sovereigns and the common folk lived in pavilions and houses of wood.

Over the half-millenia of Khmer rule, the city of Angkor became a great pilgrimage destination because of the notion of Devaraja, which was a coronation icon. Jayavarman II (802-850) was the first to use this royal icon.

The increasingly larger temples built by the Khmer kings continued to function as the locus of the devotion to the Devaraja, and were at the same time earthly and symbolic representations of mythical Mt. Meru, the cosmological home of the Hindu gods and the axis of the world-system. The symbol of the king's divine authority was the sign (*linga*) of Shiva within the temple's inner sanctuary, which represented both the axes of the physical and the psychological worlds. The worship of Shiva and Vishnu separately, and together as Harihara, had been popular for considerable time in southeast Asia; Jayavarman's chief innovation was to use ancient Vedic *mahabhisheka* to define the symbol of government.

Angkor Wat is the supreme masterpiece of Khmer art. The descriptions of the temple fall far short of communicating the great size, the perfect proportions, and the astoundingly beautiful sculpture that everywhere presents itself to the viewer. Its architecture is majestic and its representation of form and movement from Indian mythology has astonishing grace and power. The inner galleries of the temple have depiction of the battle of Kurukshetra, procession of King Suryavarman and his ministers, scenes from heavens and hells, churning of the sea of milk, the battle of Vishnu and the asuras, victory of Krishna over Bana, battle of the devas and asuras, Ravana shaking Kailasa with Shiva and Parvati atop, and the battle of Lanka between Rama and Ravana. These and other scenes are drawn with great artistic beauty. No wonder, the temple ranks amongst the greatest creations of human imagination.

To understand the astronomical aspects of Angkor Wat it is necessary to begin with the Indian traditions of altar and temple design on which it is based. And since the Angkor Wat ritual hearkened to the Vedic past, that is where we must begin. Vedic astronomy was decoded very recently. The Vedic altars had an astronomical basis related to the reconciliation of the lunar and solar years. The fire altars symbolized the universe and there were three types of altars representing the earth, the atmosphere and the sky.

The altar in its grandest form becomes the temple, now considered a representation of the Cosmic Purusha (Man), on whose body is displayed all creation in its materiality and movement. Paradoxically, the space of the Purusha is in the sanctuary only ten fingers wide, although he pervades the earth.

The temple construction begins with *the Vastupurusha mandala*, which is a yantra, mostly divided into 64 or 81 squares, which are the seats of 45 divinities. Brahma (symbolizing the origin of time) is at the center, around him 12 squares represent the Adityas (the twelve months of the year), and in the outer circle are 28 squares that represent the *nakshatras* (the constellations of the moon's orbit). The *Vastumandala* with its border is the place where the motions of the sun and the moon and the planets are reconciled. It is the Vastu in which the decrepit, old Chyavana of the Rigveda asks his sons to put him down so that he would become young again. In this story Chyavana is the moon and Sukanya, whom he desires, is the sun. Clearly, astronomy, an understanding of the physical universe, is the very basis of temple design.

The altar or the temple, as a representation of the dynamism of the universe, requires a breaking of the symmetry of the square, which stands for the heavens.

In particular, the temples to the goddess are drawn on a rectangular plan. In Shiva or Vishnu temples, which are square, change is represented by a play of diagonal lines. These diagonals are essentially kinetic and are therefore representative of movement and stress. They embody the time-factor in a composition.

Alice Boner, art-historian, writes that the Devi temples "represent the creative expanding forces, and therefore could not be logically be represented by a square, which is an eminently static form. While the immanent supreme principle is represented by the number ONE, the first stir of creation initiates duality, which is the number TWO, and is the producer of THREE and FOUR and all subsequent numbers upto the infinite."[34] The dynamism is expressed by a doubling of the square to a rectangle or the ratio 1:2, where the *garbhagriha,* the sanctum sanctorum, is now built in the geometrical centre. For a three-dimensional structure, the basic symmetry-breaking ratio is 1:2:4, which can be continued further to another doubling.

The constructions of the third millennium BC in India appear to be according to the same principles. The dynamic ratio of 1:2:4 is the most commonly encountered size of rooms of houses, in the overall plan of houses and the construction of large public buildings. This ratio is also reflected in the overall plan of the large walled sector at Mohenjo-Daro called the citadel mound. It is even the most commonly encountered brick size. Structures, dating to 2000 BC, built in the design of yantras, have been unearthed.

As a representation of the macrocosm, change in the temple is described in terms of the motions of the heavenly bodies. But the courses of the sun, the moon and the planets are unequal, so the temple design represents all characteristic time sequences: the day, the month, the year and the wider cycles marked by the recurrence of a complete cycle of eclipses.

The temple has a 1300-m north-south axis and a 1500-m west-east axis. The temple faces toward the west because that situates it to the east with respect to the worshiper, the appropriate direction for Vishnu who is a solar deity.

Various numbers from the Vedic astronomy are encountered at Angkor Wat as simple counts, or measurements in cubits, or *phyeam* = 4 cubits. Some of these represent just the basic constants of the system, while others provide specific information related to the orientation of the temple related to the nakshatras and the positions of the planets. For an example of the latter, consider that the length of the north-south axis, door to door, in the sanctuary is 13.41 cubits, which may represents the fact that the north celestial pole is 13.43 degrees above the northern horizon at Angkor. This number is also basic to the second gallery, devoted to Brahma who is "situated" at the north celestial pole.

The order in which the planets rose over the eastern horizon at the end of July 1131 is represented in the bas-relief of the northwest corner pavilion: Saturn (Agni), Jupiter (Indra), Venus (Kubera), Mars (Skanda), and Mercury (Varuna). The design of the temple can be seen in three architectural units:

1. *Central sanctuary:* Mount Meru, with 45 gods, the north celestial pole, the centre of the mandala, the spring equinox, the axis of the earth, Vishnu, Brahma, and King Suryavarman

2. *Circumferences:* the ecliptic, the moon and lunar periodicity, the constellations, the planets, the celestial year, the krita yuga, the grid of the mandala, the history of King Suryavarman

3. *Axes:* the building blocks of time (60, 108), the yuga cycles, the solar year, the lunar year, historical dates in Suryavarman's reign, the mandala and its transformation of time, and, finally, the solar year and lunar time cycles from the vantage point of Mount Meru

But astronomy only fixed the framework for the temple, the details were related to social and spiritual function. The temple was more than an observatory and ritual ground, it was also drama and dance school, the arts society, yoga academy, library, school and college and publishing house.

Angkor Wat has revealed to us the grammar of the Hindu temple. Given this knowledge, it should be possible to create new forms and designs. The modern temple will facilitate the understanding of old symbols; more importantly, it will have functions that help us fathom the mysteries of our own being.

8

The Birth of Science

I have already mentioned that the Vedic texts present a tripartite and recursive view of the physical world. The universe is viewed as three regions of earth, space, and sky which in the human being are mirrored in the physical body, the breath (prana), and mind.

In the Vedic world view, the processes in the sky, on earth, and within the mind are connected. The Vedic seers insist that all rational descriptions of the universe lead to logical paradox. The one category transcending all oppositions is *Brahman*. Understanding the nature of consciousness is of paramount importance in this view but this does not mean that other sciences are ignored. Vedic ritual is a symbolic retelling of this world view. Knowledge is classified in two ways: the lower or dual, and the higher or unified. The seemingly irreconcilable worlds of the material and the conscious are taken as aspects of the same transcendental reality.

The idea of complementarity is at the basis of the systematization of Indian philosophic traditions, so that complementary approaches are paired together. We have the groups of: logic (Nyaya) and physics (Vaisheshika), cosmology (Sankhya) and psychology (Yoga), and language (Mimamsa) and reality (Vedanta). These six views are like the six sides of a cube. Although these philosophical schools were formalized in the post-Vedic age, we find the basis of these ideas in the Vedic texts.

The Sankhya and the Yoga systems take the mind as consisting of five components: *manas, ahamkara, chitta, buddhi*, and *atman. Manas* is the lower mind which collects sense impressions. *Ahamkara* is the sense of I-ness that associates some perceptions to a subjective and personal experience. Once sensory impressions have been related to I-ness by ahamkara, their evaluation and resulting decisions are arrived at by *buddhi*, the intellect. *Chitta* is the memory bank of the mind. These memories constitute the foundation on which the rest of the mind operates. But *chitta* is not merely a passive instrument. The organization of the new impressions throws up instinctual or primitive urges which creates different emotional states. This mental complex surrounds the innermost aspect of consciousness, which is *atman* (*Self* or *Brahman*).

In this view matter appears inert only because it has not expressed its potential. By process of transformation, nature (prakriti) attains the capacity for freedom. Sentient beings are free to varying degrees.

Physics and Chemistry

The Vaisheshika system considers nine classes of substances, some of which are nonatomic, some atomic, and others all-pervasive. The nonatomic ground is provided by the three substances ether, space, and time, which are unitary and indestructible; a further four, earth, water, fire, and air are atomic composed of indivisible, and indestructible atoms; self (atman), which is the eighth, is omnipresent and eternal; and, lastly, the ninth, is the mind (manas), which is also eternal but of atomic dimensions, that is, infinitely small.

The atoms combine to form different kinds of molecules that break up under the influence of heat. The molecules come to have different properties based on the influence of various potentials (*tanmatras*). Heat and light rays are taken to consist of very small particles of high velocity. Being particles, their velocity is finite. The gravitational force was perceived as a wind. The other forces were mediated by atoms of one kind or the other.

Indian chemistry developed many different alkalis, acids and metallic salts by processes of calcination and distillation, often motivated by the need to formulate medicines. Metallurgists developed efficient techniques of extraction of metals from ore.

Geometry and Mathematics

Indian geometry began very early in the Vedic period in altar problems as in the one where the circular altar (earth) is to be made equal in area to a square altar (heavens). Two aspects of the "Pythagoras" theorem are described in the texts by Baudhayana and others. The geometric problems are often presented with their algebraic counterparts. The solution to the planetary problems also led to the development of algebraic methods.

Binary numbers were known at the time of Pingala's Chhandahshastra. Pingala, who is believed to have lived about the fifth century BC used binary numbers to classify Vedic meters. The knowledge of binary numbers indicates a deep understanding of arithmetic.

Astronomy

For many years the mainstream view was to take Indian astronomy as being essentially derivative, based on Mesopotamian and Greek sources. This view arose from the belief that the Indians did not possess a tradition of sound observation. This view was proven wrong for the Siddhantic period by Roger Billard who, using computer analysis, showed that the parameters used in the Siddhantas were accurate for the date of the texts, establishing that they couldn't have been borrowed from some old source outside of the country.

This was not accepted by all. In particular, David Pingree, who had invested his career in the paradigm that Greek astronomy was the source of Indian astronomy attacked Billard. The distinguished historian of astronomy B.L. van der Waerden stepped in as a referee. He wrote a famous paper called "Two treatises on Indian astronomy" in the *Journal for History of Astronomy* (1970), where he stated the problem as: "If Pingree is right, Billard is wrong, and conversely." Proceeding to summarize the works of each, he concluded:[35]

> Billard's methods are sound, and his results shed new light on the chronology of Indian astronomical treatises and the accuracy of the underlying observations. We also have seen that Pingree's chronology is wrong in several cases. In one case, his error amounts to 500 years … Billard's book is reliable and contains very valuable new information. I have checked several of his results, and Billard always proved right.

Meanwhile, our understanding of Vedic astronomy has changed in which my discovery of an astronomical code in the organization has played a role. These discoveries indicate that there was a long tradition of astronomical observation in India. The origins of Indian mathematics are also much ancient than previously thought.

An amulet seal from Rehman Dheri (2400 BC) indicates that the nakshatra system is an old one. The seal shows a pair of scorpions on one side and two antelopes on the other. It has been argued that this seal represents the opposition of the Orion (Mrigashiras, or antelope head) and the Scorpio (Rohini) nakshatras.

There exists another relationship between Orion and Rohini, this time the name of alpha Tauri, Aldebaran. The famous Vedic myth of Prajapati as Orion, as personification of the year, desiring his daughter (Rohini) (for example Aitareya Brahmana 3.33) represents the age when the beginning of the year shifted from Orion to Rohini. For this transgression, Rudra (Sirius, Mrigavyadha) cuts off Prajapati's head. It has been suggested that the arrow near the head of one of the antelopes represents the decapitation of Orion, and this seems a very reasonable interpretation of the iconography of the seal.

It is likely then that many constellations were named in the third millennium BC or earlier. This would explain why the named constellations in the Rigveda and the Brahmanas, such as the Rikshas (the Great Bear and the Little Bear), the two divine dogs (Canis Major and Canis Minor), the twin Asses (in Cancer), the Goat (Capricornus) and the Heavenly Boat (Argo Navis), are the same as in Europe. Other constellations described similar mythical events: Prajapati as Orion upon his beheading; Osiris as Orion when he is killed by Seth.

The Vedanga Jyotisha (VJ) of Lagadha (1300 BC) is one of the subsidiary Vedic texts, so its contents must be considered to be roughly coeval with the Brahmanas and other post-Vedic texts although the VJ text that has come down to us is definitely of a later period. The Puranas also contain a lot of very old material and their astronomy appears, on all counts, to be earlier than Aryabhata so they provide us with clues regarding the evolution of astronomical thought.

It was long popular to consider the Siddhantic astronomy of Aryabhata to be based mainly on mathematical ideas that originated in Babylon and Greece. This view was inspired, in part, by the fact that two of the five pre-Aryabhata Siddhantas in Varahamihira's Panchasiddhantika (PS), namely Romaka and Paulisha, appear to be connected to the West through the names Rome and Paul. But the planetary model of these early Siddhantas is basically an extension of the theory of the orbits of the sun and the moon in the Vedanga Jyotisha. Furthermore, the compilation of the PS occurred after Aryabhata and so the question of the gradual development of ideas can hardly be answered by examining it.

I have presented the technical details of these discoveries elsewhere. The main conclusion of these findings is that the earliest Indian astronomy is prior to the Mesopotamian one. We have traced certain Indian ideas in Mesopotamia in the second and the first millennium BC. There they were further developed and subsequently transmitted to Greece.

Using hitherto neglected texts, an astronomy of the third millennium BC has been discovered. Yajnavalkya, who perhaps lived around 1800 BC, knew of a 95-year cycle to harmonize the motions of the sun and the moon and he also knew that the sun's circuit was asymmetric.

The second millennium text Vedanga Jyotisha of Lagadha went beyond the earlier calendrical astronomy to develop a theory for the mean motions of the sun and the moon. This marked the beginnings of the application of mathematics to the motions of the heavenly bodies. An epicycle theory was used to explain planetary motions. Later theories consider the motion of the planets with respect to the sun, which in turn is seen to go around the earth.

Cosmology

The doctrine of the three constituent qualities: *sattva, rajas,* and *tamas,* plays an important role in the Sankhya physics and metaphysics. In its undeveloped state, cosmic matter has these qualities in equilibrium. As the world evolves, one or the other of these become preponderant in different objects or beings, giving specific character to each.

The recursive Vedic world-view requires that the universe itself go through cycles of creation and destruction. This view became a part of the astronomical framework and ultimately very long cycles of billions of years were assumed. Indian evolution takes the life forms to evolve into an increasingly complex system until the end of the cycle. The categories of Sankhya operate at the level of the individual as well. Life mirrors the entire creation cycle and cognition mirrors a life-history. Cosmological speculations led to the belief in a universe that goes through cycles of creation and destruction with a period of 8.64 billion years. Related to this was the notion that light traveled with a speed of 186,000 miles per second. Since these numbers were not obtained through experimentation, the accuracy of these figures must be seen as remarkable coincidence.

Grammar

Panini's grammar (5th century BC) provides 4,000 rules that describe the Sanskrit of his day completely. This grammar is acknowledged to be one of the greatest intellectual achievements of all time. The great variety of language mirrors, in many ways, the complexity of nature and, therefore, success in describing a language is as impressive as a complete theory of physics. It is remarkable that Panini set out to describe the entire grammar in terms of a finite number of rules. Scholars have shown that the grammar of Panini represents a universal grammatical and computing system. From this perspective it anticipates the logical framework of modern computers.

Medicine

Ayurveda, the Indian medicine system, is a holistic approach to health that builds upon the tripartite Vedic approach to the world. Health is maintained through a balance between three basic humors (*dosha*) of wind (vata), fire (pitta), and water (kapha). Charaka and Sushruta are two famous early physicians. Indian surgery was quite advanced. The caesarian section was known, bone-setting reached a high degree of skill, and plastic surgery was known.

The Yoga-Vasishtha

Let me take a single book, the Yoga-Vasishtha (YV), to summarize main ideas about space, time, matter, and man in the universe. The internal evidence indicates that it was authored or compiled later than the Ramayana. Scholars have dated it variously as early as first century AD or as late as the 13th or the 14th century.

YV may be viewed as a book of philosophy or as a philosophical novel. It describes the instruction given by Vasishtha to Rama, the hero of the epic Ramayana. Its premise may be termed radical idealism and it is couched in a fashion that has many parallels with the notion of a participatory universe argued by Wheeler and others. Its most interesting passages from the scientific point of view relate to the description of the nature of space, time, matter, and consciousness. It should be emphasized that the YV ideas do not stand in isolation. Similar ideas are to be found in the earlier Vedic books. At its deepest level the Vedic conception is to view reality in a monist manner; at the next level one may speak of the dichotomy of mind and matter. Ideas similar to those found in YV are also encountered in Puranas and Tantric literature.

Three kinds of motion are alluded to in the Vedic books: these are the translational motion, sound, and light which are taken to be "equivalent" to earth, air, and sky. The fourth motion is assigned to consciousness; and this is considered to be infinite in speed.

It is most interesting that the books in this Indian tradition speak about the relativity of time and space in a variety of ways. Universes defined recursively are described in the famous episode of Indra and the ants in Brahmavaivarta Purana 4.47.100-160, the Mahabharata 12.187, and elsewhere. These flights of imagination are to be traced to more than a straightforward generalization of the motions of the planets into a cyclic universe. They must be viewed in the background of an amazingly sophisticated tradition of cognitive and analytical thought.

Selected Passages

YV consists of 6 books where the sixth book itself has two parts. The numbers in the square brackets refer to the book, (part), section, verse.

Time

Time cannot be analyzed; for however much it is divided it survives indestructible. [1.23]

There is another aspect of this time, the end of action (kritanta), according to the law of nature (niyati). [1.25.6-7]

The world is like a potter's wheel: the wheel looks as if it stands still, though it revolves at a terrific speed. [1.27]

Just as space does not have a fixed span, time does not have a fixed span either. Just as the world and its creation are mere appearances, a moment and an epoch are also imaginary. [3.20]

Infinite consciousness held in itself the notion of a unit of time equal to one-millionth of the twinkling of an eye: and from this evolved the time-scale right upto an epoch consisting of several revolutions of the four ages, which is the life-span of one cosmic creation. Infinite consciousness itself is uninvolved in these, for it is devoid of rising and setting (which are essential to all time-scales), and it is devoid of a beginning, middle and end. [3.61]

Space

There are three types of space—the psychological space, the physical space and the infinite space of consciousness. [3.17]

The infinite space of undivided consciousness is that which exists in all, inside and outside … The finite space of divided consciousness is that which created divisions of time, which pervades all beings … The physical space is that in which the elements exist. The latter two are not independent of the first. [3.97]

Other universes/wormholes. I saw within [the] rock [at the edge of the universe] the creation, sustenance and the dissolution of the universe … I saw innumerable creations in the very many rocks that I found on the hill. In some of these creation was just beginning, others were populated by humans, still others were far ahead in the passage of their times. [6.2.86]

I perceived within each molecule of air a whole universe. [6.2.92]

Matter

In every atom there are worlds within worlds. [3.20]

I saw reflected in that consciousness the image of countless universes. I saw countless creations though they did not know of one another's existence. Some were coming into being, others were perishing, all of them had different shielding atmospheres (from five to thirty-six atmospheres). There were different elements in each, they were inhabited by different types of beings in different stages of evolution. [In] some there was apparent natural order in others there was utter disorder, in some there was no light and hence no time-sense. [6.2.59]

Experience

Direct experience alone is the basis for all proofs ... That substratum is the experiencing intelligence which itself becomes the experiencer, the act of experiencing, and the experience. [2.19-20]

Everyone has two bodies, the one physical and the other mental. The physical body is insentient and seeks its own destruction; the mind is finite but orderly. [4.10]

I have carefully investigated, I have observed everything from the tips of my toes to the top of my head, and I have not found anything of which I could say, 'This I am.' Who is 'I'? I am the all-pervading consciousness which is itself not an object of knowledge or knowing and is free from self-hood. I am that which is indivisible, which has no name, which does not undergo change, which is beyond all concepts of unity and diversity, which is beyond measure. [5.52]

I remember that once upon a time there was nothing on this earth, neither trees and plants, nor even mountains. For a period of eleven thousand years the earth was covered by lava. In those days there was neither day nor night below the polar region: for in the rest of the earth neither the sun nor the moon shone. Only one half of the polar region was illumined.

Then demons ruled the earth. They were deluded, powerful and prosperous, and the earth was their playground.

Apart from the polar region the rest of the earth was covered with water. And then for a very long time the whole earth was covered with forests, except the polar region. Then there arose great mountains, but without any human inhabitants. For a period of ten thousand years the earth was covered with the corpses of the demons. [6.1]

Mind

The same infinite self conceives within itself the duality of oneself and the other. [3.1]

Thought is mind, there is no distinction between the two. [3.4]

The body can neither enjoy nor suffer. It is the mind alone that experiences. [3.115]

The mind has no body, no support and no form; yet by this mind is everything consumed in this world. This is indeed a great mystery. He who says that he is destroyed by the mind which has no substantiality at all, says in effect that his head was smashed by the lotus petal … The hero who is able to destroy a real enemy standing in front of him is himself destroyed by this mind which is [non-material].

The intelligence which is other than self-knowledge is what constitutes the mind. [5.14]

Complementarity

The absolute alone exists now and for ever. When one thinks of it as a void, it is because of the feeling one has that it is not void; when one thinks of it as not-void, it is because there is a feeling that it is void. [3.10]

All fundamental elements continued to act on one another—as experiencer and experience—and the entire creation came into being like ripples on the surface of the ocean. And, they are interwoven and mixed up so effectively that they cannot be extricated from one another till the cosmic dissolution. [3.12]

Consciousness

The entire universe is forever the same as the consciousness that dwells in every atom, even as an ornament is non-different from gold. [3.4]

The five elements are the seed of which the world is the tree; and the eternal consciousness is the seed of the elements. [3.13]

Cosmic consciousness alone exists now and ever; in it are no worlds, no created beings. That consciousness reflected in itself appears to be creation. [3.13]

This consciousness is not knowable: when it wishes to become the knowable, it is known as the universe. Mind, intellect, egotism, the five great elements, and the world—all these innumerable names and forms are all consciousness alone. [3.14]

The world exists because consciousness is, and the world is the body of consciousness. There is no division, no difference, no distinction. *Hence the universe can be said to be both real and unreal: real because of the reality of consciousness which is its own reality, and unreal because the universe does not exist as universe, independent of consciousness.*} [3.14]

Consciousness is pure, eternal and infinite: it does not arise nor cease to be. It is ever there in the moving and unmoving creatures, in the sky, on the mountain and in fire and air. [3.55]

Millions of universes appear in the infinite consciousness like specks of dust in a beam of light. In one small atom all the three worlds appear to be, with all their components like space, time, action, substance, day and night. [4.2]

The universe exists in infinite consciousness. Infinite consciousness is unmanifest, though omnipresent, even as space, though existing everywhere, is manifest. [4.36]

The manifestation of the omnipotence of infinite consciousness enters into an alliance with time, space and causation. Thence arise infinite names and forms. [4.42]

Rudra is the pure, spontaneous self-experience which is the one consciousness that dwells in all substances. It is the seed of all seeds, it is the essence of this world-appearance, it is the greatest of actions. It is the cause of all causes and it is the essence of all beings, though in fact it does not cause anything nor is it the concept of being, and therefore cannot be conceived. It is the awareness in all that is sentient, it knows itself as its own object, it is its own supreme object and it is aware of infinite diversity within itself …

The infinite consciousness can be compared to the ultimate atom which yet hides within its heart the greatest of mountains. It encompasses the span of countless epochs, but it does not let go of a moment of time. It is subtler than the tip of single strand of hair, yet it pervades the entire universe …

It does nothing, yet it has fashioned the universe. All substances are non-different from it, yet it is not a substance; though it is non-substantial it pervades all substances. The cosmos is its body, yet it has no body. [6.1.36]

The YV Model of Knowledge

YV is not written as a systematic text. Its narrative jumps between various levels: psychological, social, and physical. But since the Indian tradition of knowledge is based on analogies that are recursive and connect various domains, one can be certain that our literal reading of the passages is valid.

YV appears to accept the idea that laws are intrinsic to the universe. In other words, the laws of nature in an unfolding universe will also evolve. According to YV, new information does not emerge out of the inanimate world but it is a result of the exchange between mind and matter.

It accepts consciousness as a kind of fundamental field that pervades the whole universe. One might speculate that the parallels between YV and some recent ideas of physics are a result of the inherent structure of the mind.

Other Texts

Our readings of the YV are confirmed by other texts such as the Mahabharata and the Puranas as they are by the philosophical systems of Sankhya and Vaisheshika, or the various astronomical texts.

Here is a reference to the size of the universe from the Mahabharata 12.182:[36]

> The sky you see above is infinite. Its limits cannot be ascertained. The sun and the moon cannot see, above or below, beyond the range of their own rays. There where the rays of the sun and the moon cannot reach are luminaries which are self-effulgent and which possess splendor like that of the sun or the fire. Even these last do not behold the limits of the firmament in consequence of the inaccessibility and infinity of those limits. This space which the very gods cannot measure is full of many blazing and self-luminous worlds each above the other.

The Mahabharata has a very interesting passage (12.233), virtually identical with the corresponding material in YV, which describes the dissolution of the world. Briefly, it is stated how a dozen suns burn up the earth, and how elements get transmuted until space itself collapses into wind (one of the elements). Ultimately, everything enters into primeval consciousness.

If one leaves out the often incongruous commentary on these ideas which were strange to him, we find al-Biruni in his encyclopaedic book on India written in 1030 speaking of essentially the same ideas. Here are two little extracts:[37]

> The Hindus have divided duration into two periods, a period of *motion*, which has been determined as *time*, and a period of *rest*, which can only be determined in an imaginary way according to the analogy of that which has first been determined, the period of motion. The Hindus hold the eternity of the Creator to be *determinable*, not *measurable*, since it is infinite.
>
> They do not, by the word *creation*, understand a *formation of something out of nothing*. They mean by creation only the working with a piece of clay, working out various combinations and figures in it, and making such arrangements with it as will lead to certain ends and aims which are potentially in it.

The mystery of consciousness is a recurring theme in Indian texts. Unfortunately, the misrepresentation that Indian philosophy is idealistic, where the physical universe is considered an illusion, has become very common. For an authoritative modern exposition of Indian ideas of consciousness one must turn to Aurobindo.

It appears that Indian understanding of physics was informed not only by astronomy and terrestrial experiments but also by speculative thought and by meditations on the nature of consciousness. Unfettered by either geocentric or anthropocentric views, this understanding unified the physics of the small with that of the large within a framework that included metaphysics.

This was a framework consisting of innumerable worlds (solar systems), where time and space were continuous, matter was atomic, and consciousness was atomic, yet derived from an all-pervasive unity. The material atoms were defined first by their subtle form, called *tanmatra*, which was visualized as a potential, from which emerged the gross atoms. A central notion in this system was that all descriptions of reality are circumscribed by paradox.

The universe was seen as dynamic, going through ceaseless change.

The Medieval Period

Astronomical texts called siddhantas begin appearing sometime in the first millennium BC. According to tradition there were 18 early siddhantas of which only a few have survived. Each siddhanta is an astronomical system with its own constants. Some of the famous astronomer-mathematicians that arose in India's long medieval period are listed below.

Aryabhata (born 476) took the earth to spin on its axis; this idea appears to have been his innovation. Aryabhata was aware of the relativity of motion as is clear from this passage in his book, Just as a man in a boat sees the trees on the bank move in the opposite direction, so an observer on the equator sees the stationary stars as moving precisely toward the west.

Brahmagupta, who was born in 598 in Rajasthan, wrote his masterpiece, Brahmasphuta Siddhanta, in 628. His school, which was a rival to that of Aryabhata, has been very influential in western and northern India. Brahmagupta's work was translated into Arabic in the eighth century at Baghdad and it became famous in the Arabic world as Sindhind and it influenced Islamic astronomy. One of Brahmagupta's chief contributions is the solution of a certain second order indeterminate equation which is of great significance in number theory.

Belonging to the Karnataka region, Bhaskara (born 1114), was an outstanding mathematician and astronomer. Amongst his mathematical contributions is the concept of differentials. He was the author of Siddhanta Shiromani, a book in four parts: (I) Lilavati on arithmetic, (ii) Bijaganita on algebra, (iii) Ganitadhyaya, (iv) Goladhyaya on astronomy. His epicyclic-eccentric theories of planetary motions are more developed than in the earlier siddhantas.

Subsequent to Bhaskara we see a flourishing tradition of mathematics and astronomy in Kerala which saw itself as a successor to the school of Aryabhata. Of these, Madhava (c. 1340-1425) developed a procedure to determine the positions of the moon every 36 minutes. He also provided methods to estimate the motions of the planets. He gave power series expansions for trigonometric functions, and for pi correct to eleven decimal places.

A very prolific scholar who wrote several works on astronomy, Nilakantha (c. 1444-1545) found the correct formulation for the equation of the center of the planets and his model must be considered a true heliocentric model of the solar system. He also improved upon the power series techniques of Madhava. The methods developed by the Kerala mathematicians were far ahead of the European mathematics of the day.

Another noteworthy contribution was by the school of New Logic (Navya Nyaya) of Bengal and Bihar. At its zenith during the time of Raghunatha (1475-1550), this school developed a methodology for a precise semantic analysis of language. Its formulations are equivalent to mathematical logic.

With all these brilliant achievements behind them, why didn't the Indians create a scientific revolution that touched the entire fabric of society? Clearly, the social, political and economic conditions were not ripe for such change. Europe had the advantage of the wealth obtained from the New World part of which went to the support of institutions of higher learning and the development of instruments to aid navigation.

9

Cows and Unicorns

If Indian science is much older than Greek and Babylonian science, how did the scholars of the last generation get it so wrong? When Europe began looking at India's enormous literature in the early nineteenth century, it came across material that was very old, much older than the epoch of 4004 BC when, according to the biblical account, the world had been created. So scholars considered early dates to be scarcely credible and it was decided that Indian history would be reconstructed based solely on philological research. That is like saying that only English linguistic scholars should be allowed to interpret physics books!

The theory that Indian astronomy is derived from those of the Mesopotamians and the Greeks arose from a circular logic. Indian geometry texts were dated to a period after Euclid solely on the grounds of assumed priority of Greek geometry.

A Thousand Cows, One Above the Other

The idea that Indians knew very little astronomy was considered corroborated by a passage in an ancient text called the Panchavimsha Brahmana, "The Knowledge-Book of Twenty-five Chapters," which says,

> The world of heaven is as far removed from this world as a thousand *gavah* stacked one above the other.

What does the word *gavah*, which is the plural of *gauh*, mean? Let us consult Yaska's Nirukta, the earliest book of etymology from India, It presents several primary meanings of this word in the following order (Nirukta 2.5-6):

> The planet earth

> The animal cow

Bow-string

The sun

Rays of light

Now guess which of the five meanings was used by the famed Dutch translator of this book? The *cow*! His translation reads:[38]

> The world of heaven is as far removed from this (earthly) world as a thousand cows standing the one above the other.

How do we know that this translation is wrong? If the ancients were primitive then although the statement "that the sky is one thousand cow-heights" sounds ludicrous to us, it may very well have been believed. To be sure of our meaning we must seek independent evidence from other texts. The early astronomy texts tell us that the sun (taken to be halfway to the sky) is about 500 earth-diameters from the earth, so the commonsensical meaning, the first meaning in Yaska's Nirukta, is the right one. The Greeks and the Babylonians also took the sun to be about this distance. Nevertheless, most textbooks repeat the wrong translation.

If one looks at the order in which the meaning of the term *gauh* is given, it suggests to us that the sacredness of the cow may just have symbolized the sanctity of the planet earth? The Greeks also visualized the earth as Gaia, the cow!

A Three-legged Calf

Now that we are speaking about the cow, let us also consider the famous *three-footed calf* of the Vedic times. This is the name given in the Atharvaveda 13.1.10 to the Gayatri, the most famous mantra in the Vedic corpus. Elsewhere, it is called the three-footed song or the three-footed ray of light.

This light-hearted name is to suggest that *insight* needs to be added to the symbolism and literal meaning of the mantra for it to become "four-footed" vehicle of wisdom and subtle knowledge. The mantra goes:

> *OM bhur bhuvah svah*
> *tat savitur varenyam*
> *bhargo devasya dhimahi*
> *dhiyo yonah prachodayat*

> A-u-m, earth, space, heavens (body, process, wisdom)
> That greatest Creator

We meditate upon its bright splendor
May he illumine our minds.

The *Creator* is seen as the sun of illumination in our minds *and* as transcending our selves. The Gayatri is a celebration of the power of the mind. It also tells us that there exists more than our bodies, and the mind can arrive at this larger illumination.

The Brihadaranyaka Upanishad (5.14.6-7) explains the three feet of the Gayatri: the first foot represents the three-fold division of the world; the second foot represents the three-fold knowledge of the Vedas; the third foot represents the three vital breaths (*prana*). But this knowledge, represented as a progressively deeper involution from the outer to the inner, is merely the background in which the fourth foot can be seen representing the cause and the meaning of the universe.

Unicorns

It is generally agreed that the unicorn of the Harappan iconography is a composite animal whose neck and snout resemble those of the horse or camel, while the legs are equine. The body and the tail are that of the bull.

The unicorn is a very important figure in Indian texts which points to the continuity with the Harappan period. The Puranas call Vishnu and Shiva by the name of *Ekashringa*, the "one-horned one." The Shanti-Parva (chapter 343) of the Mahabharata speaks of the one-tusked boar (Varaha) who saves the earth as Vishnu's incarnation. Here Varaha is described as being triple-humped, a figure that we see in the Harappan iconography.

In some engravings, the Harappan unicorn's horn appears to be coming out from a side. In the Sanskrit texts, we have the figure of *Shankukarna*, "one whose ear is like a nail." The Mahabharata (Vana Parva) informs that there is a temple to Shiva in the name of Shankukarna Mahadeva at the point where the river Sindhu meets the sea.

The Matsya Purana tells us that this Varaha is the same as the Vrishakapi of the Rigveda. The lexicographer Amarasimha asserts that Vrishakapi represents both Vishnu and Shiva.

Varaha, the heavenly boar-unicorn, is described in the Puranas as having muscular, round and long shoulders, a high waist, and shape of a bull. The different parts of this animal are pictured as representing the Vedas, the altar and so on. The scholar P.N. Mathur has suggested[39] that Varaha originally meant this composite unicorn and it was only later that the meaning was transferred to that of boar.

10

Light or Coincidence

Imagine that archaeologists, digging a thousand year old virgin site in Antarctica, come across an inscription deep underground that shows the sun, and next to it the numbers 300,000 kilometres per second, the speed of light. How would the world react? More likely than not, this find will not be accepted by scholars. A fraud, they would say, committed for cheap fame. The reputation of the archaeologists will be ruined.

Only lunatics will support them, claiming that this proves that aliens have visited the earth from time to time. The high priests of the academy will say that even if the find was genuine it proves nothing; at best it is a coincidence.

The speed of light was first determined in 1675 by Römer who looked at the difference in the times that light from Io, one of the moons of Jupiter, takes to reach earth based on whether it is on the near side of Jupiter or the far side. Until then light was taken to travel with infinite velocity. Even Newton assumed so.

The reason why we are talking about the absurd scenario of the archaeologists in Antarctica is because we are confronted with a situation that is quite similar!

I am an archaeologist of texts. I read old texts from the point of view of history of science. One such book is the celebrated commentary on the Rigveda by Sayana (c. 1315-1387), minister in the court of King Bukka I of the Vijayanagar Empire in South India.

In his commentary on the fourth verse of the hymn 1.50 of the Rigveda on the sun, he says:

tatha cha smaryate yojananam sahasre dve dve shate dve cha yojane ekena nimishardhena kramamana namo 'stu ta iti

Thus it is remembered: [O Sun,] bow to you, you who traverse 2,202 yojanas in half a nimesha.

This statement could either relate to the speed of the sun or to that of light. The units are well known. For example, the Puranas define 1 nimesha to be equal to 16/75 seconds; 1 yojana is about 14.4 kilometres. Substituting in Sayana's statement we get 300,000 kilometres per second.

That looks unbelievable. You'd say that it cannot be the speed of light. Maybe it refers to the speed of the sun in its supposed orbit around the earth. But that places the orbit of the sun at a distance of over 4,080 million kilometres. The correct value is only 148 million kilometres and until the time of Rőmer the distance to the sun used to be taken to be less than 6.4 million kilometres. This interpretation takes us nowhere.

What about the possibility of fraud? Sayana's statement was printed in 1890 in the famous edition of Rigveda edited by Max Műller, the German Sanskritist. He claimed to have used several three or four hundred year old manuscripts of Sayana's commentary, written much before the time of Rőmer.

Is it possible that Műller was duped by an Indian correspondent who slipped in the line about the speed? That is unlikely, because Sayana's commentary is so well known that an interpolation would have been long discovered. And soon after Műller's Rigveda was published, someone would have claimed that it contained this particular secret knowledge. The fact that the speed in the text corresponds to the speed of light was pointed out only recently. Also copies of Sayana's manuscript, dated 1395, are available.

Further support for the genuineness of the figure in the ancient book comes from one of the earliest Puranas, the Vayu, conservatively dated to at least 1,500 years old. (The same reference is to be found in the other Puranas as well.) In Chapter 50 of this book, there is the statement that the sun moves 3.15 million yojanas in 48 minutes. This corresponds to about 16,000 kilometres per second if considered as speed of light, and 216 million kilometres for the distance to the sun, if considered as the speed of the sun. Sayana's speed of light is exactly 18 times greater than this speed of the sun! Is this another coincidence?[40]

We must not forget that the Puranas speak of the creation and destruction of the universe in cycles of 8.64 billion years that is quite close to currently accepted value regarding the time of the big bang.

For the rationalists these numbers are a coincidence. But given the significance of these numbers, it is very important to look carefully at the old manuscripts of Sayana's commentary. It is also important to examine the pre-Sayana Indian astronomy theories to understand the context in which these numbers emerged.

I have come up with a plausible explanation for Sayana's number. It is based on Puranic cosmology where this speed of light appears to be the correct one to reach the furthest end of the universe within 24 hours. Obviously, if this was the explanation used, it is not correct science but it allows us to understand the framework in which Indian ideas arose.

There are others who would say that consciousness, acting on itself can find universal knowledge. Look, they'd say, by examining biological cycles one can know the periods of the sun and the moon. So why shouldn't it be possible to know other universal truths? They'd add that ancient texts speak—and this is true—of embryo transplants, multiple births from the same fetus, air and space travel, slowing or speeding of time, weapons that can destroy the entire world. They'd say that it is more than ancient science fiction, it shows that the human imagination can envision aspects of the universe by looking at itself. A case can be made that our knowledge of the outer reality is nothing but a description of the nature of the mind, because that is the instrument using which we construct our models of the outer.

In fact this is the traditional Indian view. But even if we accept its correctness, it is clear that *new* insights may be expressed only in terms of ideas and knowledge that one already possesses. So if one did somehow *see* the number 2,202, one still had to construct an explanation for this number. And this explanation could only be expressed in terms of contemporaneous science.

Lest one gets the idea that all of the speculative numbers in the Vedic texts are correct, one should point to instances where they are not right. For example, the distance of the sun from the earth (about 500 earth diameters) is off by a factor of about 20. Medieval Indian astronomy is fundamentally no more advanced compared to the Greek astronomy of its day.

But even without considering the speed of light and the age of the universe, the speculative aspect of Indian astronomy remains impressive. Puranic cosmology admits the possibility of multiple universes and many planetary systems.

The ideas regarding the distance of the sun hardly changed until the modern times.

The contradictions in the assumption that the luminaries move with uniform mean speed and the requirements imposed by the assumed size of the solar system led to a gradual enlargement of the models of the universe from about twice that of the distance of the sun in Panchavimsha Brahmana to one 4.32×10^6 times the distance of the sun by the time of Aryabhata (c. 500 AD), who makes a distinction between the distance of the sky (edge of the universe) and that of the stars which is taken to be a much smaller sixty times the distance of the sun. "Beyond the visible universe illuminated by the sun and limited by the sky is the infinite invisible universe"—this is stated in a commentary on Aryabhata's work.

The Puranic literature, part of which is contemporaneous with Aryabhata, reconciles the finite estimates of the visible universe with the old Rigvedic notion of an infinite universe by postulating the existence of an infinite number of universes.

11

The Circle of Faith

Ideas rise and fall like other living things. But with the passing of the old millennium the demise of cults and ideologies appears to have accelerated. Perhaps this quickening is due to the forces unleashed by technology. The world has become a village; time is running on fast forward.

Of what is gone, the most lamented by academics are Marxism and psychoanalysis. Many people seem to miss the neat categories that these ideologies provided. The intellectually nimble used these systems to label the world and spin out increasingly complex theses on the state of the individual or society. The rich found it spiritually satisfying to get into analysis to deal with their feelings of guilt. The demagogues found a ready recipe to seize power.

The basis to these ideologies may have been materialism, yet they provided a rich inner life to the believer. This is why there is some truth to the complaint that the postmodern world has no soul and in it style is everything. The fashion industry designs the look for tomorrow, the academic, the novelist, and the seminarian weigh in with their dogma of the year. It is quite a feat for those who crave recognition as insiders to keep up pretense of consistency in the shifting swirls of fashion.

The older times may have been simpler, but people were not any smarter. When I was at IIT Delhi, my younger sisters and brother studied at the nearby Jawaharlal Nehru University. Those were the days when SFI (the student branch of CPM) ruled the JNU Students Union. I got to know many SFI heavyweights, who have since become full-time workers of the CPM.

The belief system of the SFI members surprised me. On the one hand, they said that material basis was all to existence; on the other hand, they spoke of exploitation and suffering. They claimed to be scientific, but refused to see the deep biological basis behind human organization. They were prepared to grant the territorial instinct to birds and animals, but would not do so for humans.

Their doublespeak was astonishing. They spoke of freedom and the dictatorship of the proletariat in the same breath! Their rhetoric was about the revolution, but their strivings were for sinecures in the government and the media bureaucracy.

The believers saw nothing wrong with all this then, and perhaps they don't see anything wrong now. Many have devoted their entire lives to the cause of the Party.

This teaches us much about the human mind. Songbirds learn the songs they have heard during a critical period of their development; likewise, humans adopt, unquestioningly, ideas they come across during their impressionable years. Not all ideas are so embraced, only the ones that are properly dressed.

These ideas need not make sense to everyone. They will not be questioned even though they do not jell with reason. The core of the belief system becomes the song we hear and live our lives by. The originators of these songs are the prophets who bend the world to their will—if only transitorily. The British playwright George Bernard Shaw said aptly: "The reasonable man adapts himself to the world, the unreasonable one persists in trying to adapt the world to himself."

Not all ideologies have lost favour in the recent years, and our postmodern age has its contentious manners. If it is not race, people will struggle over what is the right way to wear a dress or shirt, or what is the right way to confront the mystery at the bottom of our hearts.

The other struggle is the old one about faith and knowledge. In Western thought, it goes back 2000 years with the Church providing a counterfoil to the idea of gnosis, which is that knowledge is possible through the psychological functions of thinking, sensation, and feeling. These functions correspond broadly to the Indic psychological terminology of sattva, rajas, and tamas, which should not surprise us since the ancient world was much more interconnected than we are willing to acknowledge.

The conscious mind is like the tip of the iceberg; below it lays the unconscious mind which is infinitely more complex. The conscious mind is the rational self and the unconscious mind is the irrational self. In India, the image used is that of an inverted tree: the conscious mind has access to just the flowers and the leaves but beyond it lies the mighty trunk and it extends as far as one can imagine.

The struggle between the conscious and the unconscious, or knowledge and faith, has taken many forms. Gnosticism went into decline in the West but modern science adopted many key elements of it. With the supersession of the Newtonian reductionism by relativity and quantum theory, more gnostic ideas have become acceptable.

But just as the old is dying, the new is being born. How do new ideas take root? How are people made to turn away from an earlier belief system? Here it is instructive to read the well-documented accounts of the rise of Marx, Lenin, Freud, Hitler, and Mao. For greater historical distance, the Catholic Church presents an excellent case study.

In his very perceptive book, *Psychological Types,* Carl Jung discusses Tertullian and Origen, two major figures in the creation of the Church. They were born in about 160 and 185 in Carthage and Alexandria, respectively. Jung sees these two individuals as poles apart, reacting to the Gnostic tradition in different ways—Tertullian as an introvert and Origen as an extrovert. Both had to deny something in order to make sense of their belief system. For Tertullian, it was the inner reality, for Origen it was the outer world.

Jung says this about Tertullian:[41]

> To him is ascribed the sublime confession: *Credo quia absurdum est,* I believe because it is absurd. This does not altogether accord with historical fact, for he merely said: "And the Son of God died, which is immediately credible because it is absurd. And buried he rose again, which is certain because it is impossible."

Origen, on the other hand, castrated himself. He did this extreme act to get rid of the guilt about his sexuality since the Church ideology demanded a complete abolition of the sensual aspect of knowing. In order to fight the prevailing Gnostic system which believed in the possibility of knowing the world through thought, sensation, and feeling, the Church responded by rejecting the first two and preserved only feeling, which was to be centered in faith.

Tertullian performed self-mutilation via *sacrificium intellectus* that led him to an unqualified recognition of the irrational inner reality, the true rock of this faith. Origen was led to *sacrificium phalli* to sunder the strongest sensual tie to the object, in his case the most valuable function related to the perpetuation of the race.

It was the audacity of their acts that made Tertullian and Origen figures of myth and veneration.

The sacrifices of Tertullian and Origen may appear irrelevant to our times. But they offer a great lesson on the process of creation of myth and ideology. It is often the bizarre that is at the foundation of the mainstream ideology.

We can't even begin to imagine what, unbeknownst to us, is being born in our midst. We can't imagine what circles are being drawn by faith.

12

Rhythms and the Inner World

Our feeling that we perform better at certain times is no superstition. Our lives are indeed governed by inner clocks. Our blood pressure, body temperature, mental performance have cyclic patterns over the day; we have greater threshold to pain in the afternoon. Drugs are more effective at certain hours of the day. Some sleep disorders and serious psychiatric problems arise due to a malfunctioning of the inner clocks.

If our daily moods are governed by the motions of the Sun and the Moon, then do the wanderings of the planets also have a like influence? We perceive the physical world through our senses. This could be possible only if the complexity of our cognitive system equaled the complexity of the outer world. No wonder that the brain is as complex as the entire physical universe. In fact the number of stars and the number of neurons in the brain are both estimated to be about a thousand billion or 10^{12}.

A source of great wonder is how living creatures or even the cells within a body all perform in such perfect unison so that no machine can match the process. The materialist position cannot explain biological intelligence; the most powerful computers cannot do what is natural to life. For example, moving is easy for animals, even those with very small brains. But robots, in spite of all their computing resources, cannot move in natural environments. Each living organism is perfectly suited to perform in its environment. Since this environment has a rhythmic character one would expect that the behavior of all animals and plants and also the cells within each organism will also have a corresponding rhythmic nature.

The connections between the external and the internal worlds described in the Vedas make us ask: Are the luminaries of the hymns situated in the sky or in the firmament of our inner landscapes or both? The answer to this question is *yes*. The connection between the inner and the outer luminaries is the heart of Jyotisha.

We find the same thing in other cultures. These connections were expressed in mythological stories. The mythical heroes may have been anthropomorphised but knowledgeable people knew that they represented the stars and forces within the individual.

It is for this reason why pre-modern astronomers were also astrologers but by the Middle Ages the basic idea of the commonality of rhythms had been lost. The other ancient notion is of a metaphorical journey from the physical body to the golden center of consciousness. When the idea was taken literally, it became alchemy.

Many scientists in the Middle Ages were alchemists. By this time, the intervening Christian centuries had caused the true meaning of mind and spirit being the *golden* center of being to have been forgotten.

Even Newton was an alchemist and he spent more years doing his alchemy than science. This is how John Maynard Keynes characterized Newton:[42]

> Newton was not the first of the Age of Reason. He was the last of the magicians, the last of the Babylonians and Sumerians, the last great mind which looked out on the visible and intellectual world with the same eyes as those who began to build our intellectual world rather less than 10,000 years ago … Why do I call him a magician? Because he looked on the whole universe and all that is in it as a *riddle*, as a secret which could be read by applying pure thought to certain evidence, certain mystic clues which God had laid about the world to allow a sort of philosopher's treasure hunt to the esoteric brotherhood. He believed that these clues were to be found partly in the evidence of the heavens and in the constitution of the elements (and that is what gives the false suggestion of his being an experimental natural philosopher), but also partly in certain papers and traditions handed down by the brethren in an unbroken chain back to the original cryptic revelation. Newton's efforts turned out to be confused and he wasted all his later years experimenting on how to turn mercury into gold and similar projects.

The word planet is akin to the Greek *planēt-*, wanderer, that speaks to the motion of these bodies against the background of stars. The ancients spoke of the seven planets: Sun, Moon, Mercury, Venus, Mars, Jupiter, and Saturn. If there exist counterparts to the physical planets in our inner world then it is natural to expect planetary periods to show up in the patterns of our lives. Astrology, in its purest form, is just a description of the planetary periods on the life cycle of an individual.

To the question asked by the skeptic on how can the motions of an object, millions of kilometres away, have any influence on the life of a human being one can only say that the universe is interconnected. In this ecological perspective the physical planets do not influence the individual directly. Rather, the intricate clockwork of the universe runs on forces that are reflected in the periodicities of the astral bodies as also the cycles of behaviors of all terrestrial beings and plants.

It is not the gravitational pull of the planet that causes a certain response, but an internal clock governed by the genes. We know this because in some mutant organisms the internal clock works according to periods that have no apparent astronomical basis. These cycles can be considered to be a manifestation of the motions of the body's inner planets. In the language of evolution theory one would argue that these periods get reflected in the genetic inheritance of the biological system as a result of the advantage over millions of years that they must have provided for survival.

Rhythms of Life

The most fundamental rhythms are matched to the periods of the Sun or the Moon. For example, the potato has a variation in its metabolic processes that is matched to the sidereal day, the 23-hour 56-minute period of rotation of the earth relative to the fixed stars.

Various flowers open and close at particular times of the day and Carolus Linnaeus (1707-1778), the Swedish botanist, devised a flower clock based on this fact.

When plucked and placed in a vial of sugar water solution, a single flower will continue to open and close on its native period. Likewise, a single leaf will also continue to show its rhythmic up-down behavior. The clock is thus distributed all over the plant.

The cicadas come in many species including ones that appear yearly in midsummer. The best known amongst the others are those that have 13-year and 17-year periods. The North American 17-year cicada spends 17 years as a juvenile form or nymph feeding underground on the sap of plant roots. Adults emerging from these nymphs in the same year spend a summer of song and mate and the females lay their eggs. The young nymphs that hatch out burrow underground and disappear for the next 17 years.

Biological clocks come in various cycles: the 24-hour daily cycle of the Sun; 24 hour 50 minute cycle of the Moon and its half, 12 hour 25 minutes, which is also the period of the tides; 29.5 days which is the period from one new Moon to another, the yearly cycle of the Sun, and certain multiples of the year that have astronomical significance. These show up in the life cycles of many marine plants and of animals. Astrologers claim that there are others that correspond to the periods of the planets or the periods of their conjunctions.

There are other cycles such as the 11-year sunspot cycle and its double the 22-year magnetic cycle. There is a well-documented correlation between this and the 22-year cycle of drought in the Western United States. The interval between two perfectly straight alignments between the Earth, the Moon, and the Sun responsible for the solar eclipse cycle is 18.6 years. This period is also the drought cycle of the American Midwest east of the Rockies and west of the Mississippi.

Fiddler crabs, in their natural habitat on the shore, burrow themselves during high-tide, emerging when the tide recedes to feed, mate, and challenge each other.

When these crabs are removed to the laboratory and held in an incubator with constant conditions, they still run around in their containers during the time of each low tide. According to one scientist, "So accurate are their responses that the students working in the lab use the crab behavior patterns, rather than the tide tables of the Geodetic Survey, to plan their field trips to the crab's old home 30 miles across Cape Cod … How do crabs do it? It is not yet known."[43] Crabs are not unique at this; all living creatures have extremely precise inner cycles.

In humans the menstrual period has by tradition been taken to correspond to the Moon's motion; in fact "menses" means lunar month. New research supports this:

> In a study of a number of women with variable onset of menstrual periods, artificial illumination of the bedroom through the 14th to 17th nights following the onset of menstruation resulted in the regularization of the period, with the period length coming very close to 29.5 days, the natural synodic month. That this period is a biologically significant one for the human species is further suggested by the fact that the average duration of pregnancy (from ovulation to birth) in the human is rather precisely nine 29.53 synodic months.
> *Encyclopaedia Britannica* (1994)

There is a distinction between lunar and freerunning circalunar cycles. A lunar cycle is in step with the motions of the Moon. The menstrual cycle is a freerunning cycle with the same period as that of the Moon. One might assume that entrainment to the lunar cycle was triggered by moonlight. In the living under artificial lights of modern times it is easy to see how the direct correlation with the Moon's motion has been lost.

It is surprising that the fundamental circadian rhythm inside us is not the 24-hour one related to the motion of the Sun but rather the 24 hour 50 minute one according to the period of the Moon. We share this approximately 25-hour clock with monkeys and other non-humans. Since then it has been found that our inner clock is synchronized with the motions of the Moon and it is reset continually by sunlight.

This 25-hour clock was discovered by the moderns only about 30 years ago in experiments on a blind squirrel monkey. The activity of this monkey were recorded night and day for a period of three years and it was discovered that her rhythms drifted later each day by an average of about 46 minutes. Was the deficit of four minutes from the moonrise period due to the reference with respect to the stars, we do not know. The monkey kept her own time, unaffected by the activities around her.

Part of our intellectual quest is to understand our ancient literature. It is reasonable to assume that with their emphasis on time bound rituals and the calendar, the ancients had discovered many of the biological periods. This would include the 25-hour circadian rhythm, the connection of the menstrual cycle with the motions of the Moon, the life cycles of various plants, and the semi-monthly estrus cycle of sheep, the three-week cycles of cattle and pigs, and the six-month cycle of dogs. Perhaps they knew other planetary cycles as well and some passages in the old literature hint at these connections.

The ancient world used the lunar calendar widely, especially in India and Babylon. Apart from biological rhythms of the human and astronomical cycles, we suspect that ancient understanding was also influenced by rhythms of the kind seen in the deep-sea lily near Japan:

> This echinoderm liberates its sex cells once every year in October at about 3 PM on the day of one of the Moon's quarters. In succeeding years the time of sex cell release changes, among the Moon's two quarters, first-third-first, to progressively slightly earlier dates in October. The triplets are repeated until about the first of the month whereupon the following year it jumps abruptly to near the end of the month to start the advancing triplet progression again. The result is an 18-year cycle, which is essentially the period of regression of the Moon's orbital plane. *Encyclopaedia Britannica* (1994)

The ancients further assumed that there were less obvious cycles that were matched to the motions of the other heavenly bodies.

Gestation Periods

The gestation periods for mammals also have intriguing relationships to astronomical numbers. Perhaps such connections were the basis for marking out certain animals as special symbols. The averages of some of the gestation periods are:

ass	365 days
sacred baboon	183 days
cow	284 days
dog	61 days
horse	336 days
human	284 days
rabbit	31 days

It is no wonder, then, that the ass is used as a symbol for the year in an ancient Indian text. Likewise the horse with its average gestation period equal to the nakshatra year of 336 days (for 28 nakshatras) is a natural symbol for the year in the context of the nakshatras and this we do find in the texts. The gestation period for the baboon, held sacred by the Egyptians, is exactly half of the solar year. That the gestation periods for the human and the cow are about the same is one reason for the sacredness assigned to the cow. Knowledge of biological periods appears to have played a role in the choice of some as sacred symbols.

Yoga

There are many clues that imply that the ancients had a very sophisticated attitude to the inner rhythms. I have mentioned that the ancient Indian calendar is an attempt to harmonize the motions of the Sun and the Moon. Further, it is clear that the Indians were aware of the predominant influence of the Moon on human behavior. Yoga may be seen as the harmonization of the motions of the *inner planets* of the body.

Patanjali's Yoga Sutra speaks of how meditation on the Sun reveals the nature of the world-system and meditation on the Moon and the Polestar reveals the arrangement and the motion of the planets and the stars. Such assertions imply that turning inward can provide insights.

In mantra meditation a simple syllable is repeated to achieve a rhythmic self-centeredness to establish contact with the rhythms of the cosmos.

In Chinese medicine, the subtle rhythms of our consciousness are assumed to arise out of the dynamic interplay of yin and yang and through the vibrating energy of *chi*. Chi is taken to circulate round the body in 24 hours and in a healthy person the chi of the body is in harmony with the chi of the environment. In Ayurveda, the inner rhythms arise from an interplay between three humors. There is no real difference between yin-yang and the Ayurvedic categories of rajas-tamas. It is the additional category of sattva in Ayurveda which sets humans apart from animals. Sattva provides a transcendence beyond the usual dynamics established by opposites.

Many activities are pleasurable because they make us aware of our inner rhythms. Sexual intercourse is only one window to these rhythms. Others are music, dancing, singing, and mantra meditation.

Modern customs are based only on the demands of the material body. In the ancient times when a loved one passed away, there was year-long grieving. Recent studies show that the unconscious of those who are left behind—as demonstrated by the content of dreams—does require about a year to accept the departure. It is accurate to say that from the point of view of the living the subtle person lives on for some more time.

Cycles in Ancient India

Fire, having become speech, entered the mouth
Air, becoming scent, entered the nostrils
The Sun, becoming sight, entered the eyes
The Regions becoming hearing, entered the ears
The plants, becoming hairs, entered the skin
The Moon, having become mind, entered the heart.

Aitareya Aranyaka

This verse from the Upanishadic period speaks at many levels. At the literal level there is an association of the elements with various cognitive centers. At another level, the verse connects the time evolution of the external object to the cognitive center.

Fire represents consciousness and this ebbs and flows with a daily rhythm. Air represents seasons so here the rhythm is longer. The Sun and sight have a 24-hour cycle. The Regions denote other motions in the skies so hearing manifests cycles that are connected to the planets. The plants have daily and annual periods; the hairs of the body have an annual period. The mind has a period of 24 hours and 50 minutes like that of the Moon.

According to yoga the chakras of the body are the centers of the different elements as well as cognitive capacities and rhythms related to internal planets:

Muladhara	earth	smell	Saturn
Svadhishthana	water	taste	Jupiter
Manipura	fire	sight	Mars
Anahata	air	touch	Venus
Vishuddha	ether	hearing	Mercury
Ajna	mind	thought	Moon and Sun

The yogi wishes to get in tune with the source of these rhythms. By practiced repetition of a sound and by stilling the noise within the mind, he (or she) is able to get in tune with the rhythms of the material and the subtle selves. Once that happens, it is believed the yogi is close to fathoming the mystery of time and consciousness.

Although the chakras are traditionally shown to exist down the spine, we do know that all parts of the body are mapped into corresponding centers in the brain. The ascent through the chakras is a journey through brain centers that provides illumination and mastery.

Consider just the Ajna chakra, the center of the "third eye." In birds, the pineal gland at the top of the brain is believed to be location of the clock controlling the bird's circadian rhythms. This third eye for birds is sensitive to light and its removal makes the bird's behavior arhythmic. In humans such a third eye is believed to reside in the hypothalamus in the mid-brain near abouts the Ajna chakra. The primary clock here controls body functions such as temperature, metabolic rate, appetite and thirst. The primary clock is adjusted to daylight by a specific input from the eyes that has nothing to do with normal vision.

Current scientific research on inner cycles has synthesized information in terms of averages. We don't know what the significance of the departure from these averages is for a specific individual.

The ancient world recognized that man's unique capacity for introspection gave him an opportunity to understand and master these cycles. A person's *dharma* is to know the nature of one's being, one's rhythms. No particular dharma is superior to another, each is a part of the great cosmic game.

Paradoxically, once in tune with the inner rhythms one is able to transcend the causal links that establish this behavior. This is why yogis have such mastery over their personal selves.

Our jobs, the cultural milieu, the cities we live in, define their own rhythms. We face enormous pressures to conform to these rhythms, to become a cog in the wheel of society. The challenge of life is not to surrender our personal rhythms to those that resonate around us. Rather, we should interact with the world in a creative dance where each one of us is able to maintain his own unique role. Seemingly marching to different drummers we are, nevertheless, part of a magnificent cosmic dance.

13

The Dance of Shiva

Who is Shiva? And what is the meaning of the *shivalinga*, Shiva's symbol or icon? Who is Parvati? Why do people go on pilgrimage to places like the Amaranath cave in Kashmir? What is the relationship between Shiva and Vishnu? What is the meaning of Shiva's dance?

In the Vedic way God, or *Brahman*, is perceived as being beyond logical and associational categories. That is why it is viewed as the entity that has all attributes or is beyond all attributes! But it assumes various forms when the context of the inquiry is limited. This is how a single all-pervading, omniscient entity takes many forms and comes to have many names. Each name is a *deva*, a bright point of consciousness that represents different angles to the same effulgence! These devas reside within us and also without.

The essence of the tradition is knowledge. Veda means knowledge. And the tradition is called *vaidika*, "Vedic," or equivalently *Arya Dharma*, "the noble way," *Satya Dharma*, "the way of the truth," or *Sanatana Dharma*, "the eternal way." God or Brahman are synonymous with truth. Ordinary knowledge is paradoxical because it is limited knowledge. On the other hand, true knowledge cannot be apprehended in terms of conditioned experience or language.

Symbols are used to represent transcendental notions of reality and existence. But it is understood that these symbols are only to help one obtain this experience. These symbols must be infused with movement since the underlying reality is that of change.

The Atharvaveda has a very famous hymn (10.7) which throws light on the mystery of Shiva. This is the hymn to *skambha*, the cosmic frame or pillar of creation. This is the pillar which gives a unity to the creation. It may also be visualized as the axis around which the stars move.

> In what member (of the frame) rests the earth? Where is the atmosphere? Where is the sky set? Where is situated what is beyond the sky?

The skambha sustains both heaven and earth here; the skambha sustains the wide space;
The skambha sustains the six wide directions; into the skambha has entered this whole existence.

The universe, seen as being woven together and interconnected, has an invisible axis (pillar) around which the stars move; likewise, the unity of our experience is established by the axis of consciousness to which we bind our associations. This axis is taken to be universal—it is the same for all sentient beings.

Vishnu, the pervader, represents the mystery of the physical universe; Shiva is the axis of our consciousness. They are really not distinct since the physical universe can be apprehended only through consciousness, and consciousness requires physical support. This is expressed in the Harihara form which is half Vishnu and half Shiva. As sentient beings our consciousness is primary, which is what makes Shiva the *Ishvara* (the enjoyer) or *Maheshvara* (the great lord).

chaitanyatsarvamutpannam jagadetaccharacaram

All this universe, movable or immovable, has come out of intelligence.
—*Shiva Samhita*

In their fundamental conception Shiva and Vishnu represent complementarity. Nevertheless, over the centuries, each has come to represent both the aspects of separation and union.

The creation of the universe is mirrored in the creation of each moment. To move on we must destroy. That is why we must make the supreme sacrifice of our own current state before we can fashion ourselves in a new image. The Vedic way is the way of transformation, of finding the perfect being in our selves.

There are three dances associated with Shiva. The first is a dance in the Himalayas of our beings, watched by the devas; this is the ordinary play of consciousness. This represents the movement of consciousness at the societal level. The second is his *tandava* dance in the form of Bhairava; this marks the end of one creation, one life, one universe. Thirdly, as a more explicit image is the dance of Shiva as Nataraja, the lord of dancers, in the golden hall of the Chidambaram, the center of the universe in the sky of the mind, in the heart of the temple.

The dance of Shiva represents five activities (*panchakritya*): *srishti* (creation, evolution), *sthiti* (preservation, support), *samhara* (destruction), *tirodhana* (veiling), and *anugraha* (grace). These activities of the Supreme are mirrored in the consciousness of the individual also.

Creation arises from the drum; protection proceeds from the hand of hope; from fire, held in the other hand, proceeds destruction; the foot held aloft gives release. Shiva himself is shown poised within a fiery arch. The arch represents matter, nature (prakriti), and Shiva, dancing within the arch, is the universal spirit (purusha).

Ananda Coomaraswamy summarizes the essential significance of the dance thus:

> First, it is the image of his rhythmic play as the source of all movement within the cosmos, which is represented by the arch; secondly, the purpose of his dance is to release the countless souls of men from the snare of illusion; thirdly, the place of the dance, *chidambaram,* the centre of the universe, is within the heart.[44]

During the Rigvedic time the common name of Shiva was Rudra. Yaska in his Nirukta says that Rudra is so called because he roars (*rauti*), or because he runs (*dravati*). The roaring is to remind us that in spite of ceaseless change we are the same person, and the running is the motion of our awareness.

The Nirukta also describes Rodasi, symbolizing heaven and earth or all creation, as the wife of Rudra. The universe exists because we can observe it!

Parvati is the individual intelligence that must strive to unite with the cosmic intelligence. Intelligence is likened to a flash of lightning which is why Parvati is represented as being white, the daughter of Himalaya, the mountain which is chitta, the repository of associations—memory.

Shiva as the Lord of Yoga

Shiva represents the tensions and the oppositions that lie at the basis of cognition, of creation. On the one hand, consciousness must focus entirely on the subject; and on the other hand, it must define itself in relation to the rest. How are such contrasts achieved?

There are two ways we can approach reality. We can either *be*, or *become*, or more commonly, be in a constant vortex of *becoming*. If we accept ourselves as who we think we are then our relationship with the rest of the universe has a fundamental divide: the divide of *I* and *It*. Comprehension can only proceed by reflecting on the rhythms of nature. This is the path of outer science or that of analysis. If we accept the proposition that our subjective impressions are merely a representation in terms of associational categories of a transcendental reality, then we can hope to transform ourselves into a reasonable simulacrum of this reality.

Since this reality includes us, we can hope to be transmuted into it. The way of this change—this enlargement—is the yogic way. Shiva, as the representation of this transcendental reality, is the self we seek to return to. Shiva is the inner lord who makes yoga possible.

Parenthetically, it should be noted that bhakti and yoga are the same. Bhakti arises from the root *bhaj*, "to separate," "to divide." The original idea in bhakti was to meditate on the apparent reasons for our feelings of "separateness" from our transcendental self that helps, in a counter-intuitive way, to a merger. The feeling of separateness was heightened through a remembering of mythical episodes or relating one's existential aloneness to a longing for fullness.

Of Many Gods

Other traditions also speak of a similar comprehensive view of reality. For example, in Pancharatra a cosmological system is built around Vasudeva-Krishna (Vishnu). From Vasudeva, identified as the transcendental consciousness, develops Sankarshana (Balarama), who represents primal matter. In turn, the two produce Pradyumna (mind) and Aniruddha (ahamkara or self-consciousness).

The dance of Shiva is then no different from the cosmic play of Krishna. Shiva-Krishna or whatever other name you use for it, resides in each heart. The dance is recreated in each moment and across ages. Indra's pole, Shiva's *linga*, or Krishna's flute are each the same anchor which allows us to be whole.

This dance is expressed in many ways in human contexts. Such expression appears to represent the fundamental archetypes of human consciousness. We see it in a variety of art, poetry, and music. We take two examples from Indian poetry where the divine is compared to the lover one is pining for.

The 7th century playwright and poet, Bhavabhuti, describes the love between Rama and Sita as capturing the love for the individual for the divine:

> When we talked at random—
> our cheeks pressed close together,
> > deep in love
> softly, oh softly
> of something unspeakable,
> our arms busy in close embrace
> only the darkness ended—
> the night-watches passed unnoticed.

The Vaishnava poet Yadunatha expresses his feelings for Krishna in the following manner:

> As water is to the creatures of the sea and nectar to the chakora bird; as night is companion to the stars, so is my love to Krishna. As the image in the mirror is to the body, so am I to Krishna. My life is marked deeply with his mark just as the moon is forever marked. A day without the sun, so is my heart without my lord. Yadunatha says, Cherish this and keep it young, O lucky girl who deeply loves.

The emotions raised in the separation songs of Vishnu are personal, because Rama or Krishna are, after all, human. The relationship with Shiva is more abstract, unless one meditates on the allegory of the love of Parvati for Shiva.

Artistic Expressions

Ultimately, all abstract conceptions must be reduced to images. The temple is an attempt to reduce the abstract equations to form. The entire universe is pictured in the Vedas as the body of purusha—the primal god. Or it is pictured as a temple. This may be reduced to the equation that the human body—through which we apprehend the universe—is a temple.

The poet Basavanna says,

> The rich will make temples for Shiva, What shall I, a poor man, do? My legs are pillars, the body the shrine, the head the cupola of gold. Listen, O lord of the meeting rivers, things standing shall fall, but the moving ever shall stay.

At a more practical level, any place that elicits the feeling of wonder and awe is a temple. This is why the whole experience of the journey to the cave of Amaranath was associated with Shiva: it is like the wondrous journey of the individual towards self-knowledge. In our times, the great national parks, like the Grand Canyon or the Zion in America, the vastnesses of the tableland near Kailasa, the charming Himalayan valleys, or scenic spots everywhere in the world serve as temples.

Parvati will find her Shiva and there will be a wedding of the two, when we think of ourselves from afar. More immediately, each gopi (the personal incomplete self) will pine for Krishna, the masterly flute player!

14

The Church and the Temple

When French missionaries, Hac and Gabet, visited Lhasa in 1842, they were astonished by how similar Buddhist ritual was to the Catholic: "The crozier, the mitre, the chasuble, the cardinal's robe, the double choir at the Divine Office, the chants, the exorcism, the censer with five chains, the blessing which the Lamas impart by extending the right hand over the heads of the faithful, the rosary, the celibacy of the clergy, their separation from the world, the worship of saints, the fasts, processions, litanies, holy water—these are the points of contact which the Buddhists have with us."[45]

Historians have been aware of these similarities for a long time. Some have argued that the early Christian ritual was born out of the then prevailing religious practices in the Near East and Buddhism may have served as the prototype.

Others have suggested that these parallels arise from Jesus having lived in India during his missing years of youth. This theory was presented by the Russian journalist Niclas Notovitch in his book *Unknown Life of Jesus Christ* over a hundred years ago. Having read this book carefully, I concur with the scholarly opinion that it is a forgery. Neither have we seen any other credible evidence establishing the presence of Jesus in India.

A variant of the previous theory is that Jesus did not die at the crucifixion, and he returned to India where he lived to a ripe old age in Kashmir, It has been promoted by (i) Ahmediyyas, to make the point that by his life in India, Jesus, a Biblical prophet, paved the way for the later Ghulam Ahmed, and by (ii) New-Agers, who wish to show that Christianity's spiritual basis was directly derived from Jesus's visit to India. This theory is given even less credence by scholars.

Some scholars even dispute the existence of Jesus as there is no mention of him in Roman records of the time. The first reference to Jesus is in a letter by Paul written in 55 AD, which has prompted the claim that Christianity is Paul's creation. The Dead Sea scrolls have raised further questions regarding this early history.

To explain the parallels, the historian H.G. Rawlinson suggested[46] a borrowing from Buddhism by Christianity of the ideas of miraculous conception and birth, the star over the birthplace, the prophecy of the aged Asita (the Buddhist Simeon), the temptation by Mara, the twelve disciples, and the miracles. He thinks that the rosary, the veneration of relics, and the exaggerated forms of asceticism in Christianity are from Indian sources.

We also know that early Christianity accepted reincarnation. Orthodox Christianity took many centuries to form and as the discovery in 1945 of the gnostic gospels at Nag Hammadi demonstrates, the later Church departed in many ways from the original beliefs of the community.

Here we speak of architecture of sacred space and its ritual. In particular, we wish to examine the prehistory of the temple before the Buddhist times.

Temples, as sacred spaces, are found in all ancient cultures. The parallels between the ancient temples of India and Greece (for example, Delphi in Greece and pilgrimage centers described in the Puranas) may be due to mutual borrowings, evolution from a common heritage, or a consequence of universal archetypes.

There is ample evidence of trade and interaction between the West and India going back to the third millennium BC. The Sumerians looked east for their spiritual homeland and Indus seals have been found in Mesopotamia. There is evidence of the Indic element in West Asia in the second millennium BC.

The Hindu Temple

For the clearest articulation of the philosophy behind temple design we must turn to Indic sources. According to the Sthapatya Veda (the Indian tradition of architecture), the temple and the town should mirror the cosmos. The temple architecture and the city plan are, therefore, related in their conception. There exists continuity in the Indian architectural tradition. The Harappan cities have a grid plan, just as is recommended in the Vedic manuals. The square shape represents the heavens, with the four directions representing the cardinal directions as well as the two solstices and the equinoxes of the sun's orbit.

A late example of a city designed according to the Vedic precepts is Jaipur. Vidyadhara, who designed the plan of the city, used the *pithapada* mandala as the basis. In this mandala of nine squares that represents the universe, the central square is occupied by the earth. In the city, which consists of nine large squares, the central square is assigned to the royal palace. The astronomical monuments of Maharaja Jai Singh II may also be seen as embodiments of the Vedic altars.

The Hindu temple represents the Meru mountain, the navel of the earth. The Brihat Samhita lists the many design requirements that the temple building must satisfy. For example, it says "the height of the temple should be double its width, and the height of the foundation above the ground with the steps equal to a third of this height. The *sanctum sanctorum* should be half the width of the temple" and so on. It also lists twenty types of temples that range from one to twelve storeys in height.

Temple Antecedents

The temple is considered in the image of the Cosmic Purusha, on whose body is displayed all creation in its materiality and movement. The prototype of the temple is the *Agnikshetra,* the sacred ground on which the Vedic altars are built, which is an oblong or trapezoidal area. It has been suggested that the agnichayana sacred ground is the prototype, because in it is installed a golden disc (*rukma*) representing the sun with a golden image of the purusha on it. The detailed ritual includes components that would now be termed Shaivite, Vaishnava, or Shakta. In the Nachiketa Agni, 21 bricks of gold are placed one top of the other in a form of shivalinga. The disk of the *rukma,* which is placed in the navel of the uttaravedi (the main altar) on a lotus leaf is in correspondence to the lotus emanating from Vishnu's navel which holds the universe. Several bricks are named after goddesses, such as the seven krittikas.

The temple is the representation of the cosmos both at the level of the universe and the individual, making it possible for the devotee to get inspired to achieve his own spiritual transformation.

Complementing the tradition of the Vedic ritual was that of the *munis* and yogis who lived in caves and performed austerities. From this tradition arose the Vihara, where the priests lived and the chaitya halls that also housed the stupa paralleling the uttaravedi. The rock-cut chaityas represent a surviving form of a tradition that was usually implemented using wood or brick. The later temple tradition is linked to the rock-cut chaityas and other wooden chaityagrihas.

The Ashtadhyayi of Panini (5th/4th century BC) has a clear mention of images. The ordinary images were called pratikriti and the images for worship were called archa (As. 5.3.96-100). Patanjali, the 2nd century BC author of the Mahabhashya commentary on the Ashtadhyayi, tells us more about the pratikriti and archa.

Amongst other things we are told that a toy horse is called ashvaka. (This means that the queen who lay down with the ashvaka in the Ashvamedha did not sleep with the dead horse.) Deity images for sale were called Shivaka etc, but an archa of Shiva (Rudra of the earlier times) was just called Shiva. Patanjali mentions Shiva and Skanda deities. There is also mention of the worship of Vasudeva (Krishna). We are also told that some images could be moved and some were immoveable. Panini also says that an archa was not to be sold and that there were people (priests) who obtained their livelihood by taking care of it. Panini and Patanjali mention temples that were called prasadas. There is no mention of the term mandira.

The design of the chaitya is a forerunner to the design of a cathedral. Some see the chaitya as being derived from the Lycian temple, but its evolution from the Vedic altar-complex appears more natural. The chaitya hall that housed the stupa may be seen as a development out of the agnichayana tradition where within the brick structure of the altar were buried the rukma and the golden purusha. The image is placed in a perforated brick that encases it like a casket quite like the casket of the stupa with the relic within it.

The rock-cut temples preserve features of earlier structures that have not survived. For example, we see the pointed arch of the chaitya halls that is not seen in other monuments on the ground made of brick or stone until the 8th or 9th century. In the words of the art-historian Susan Huntington regarding the Mauryan-period Lomash Rishi cave: "The sophisticated woodworking techniques recorded in the cave makes it certain that ancient India had an elaborate and lengthy history of wooden architecture prior to the Maurya period, though some of the forms are only preserved then."

The temple represents the outer and the inner cosmos. The outer cosmos is expressed in terms of various astronomical connections between the temple structure and the motions of the sun, the moon, and the planets. The inner cosmos is represented in terms of the consciousness at the womb of the temple and various levels of the superstructure that correspond to the states of consciousness.

The Buddhist temple and the Catholic cathedral do not consciously express the same range of details about the cosmos, but they are also meant to represent the heavens. Vedic philosophy and ritual helps us understand the symbols behind the Buddhist and Catholic ritual. For example, it explains why the rosary has 108 beads. For this no satisfactory explanation is provided within the Christian tradition.

15

The Vedic Religion in Ancient Iran

Scholars generally agree that before the advent of Zarathushtra, the religion of the devas was current in Iran. For want of a better term, some have called the pre-Zoroastrian religion Persian paganism. But here we argue that to do so is to obscure its connections with the Vedic religion. The similarities between the pre-Zoroastrian Persian religion and the Vedic religion are too many to give it any other name.

The term Zoroastrian is after the Greek version of the name of the prophet Zarathushtra (zarat, like Sanskrit *harit*, golden; *ushtra*, Sanskrit or Old Persian for camel) who has been variously estimated to have lived either around the time 1200 BC or perhaps half a millennium later. A Greek tradition assigns him to an age 258 years prior to Alexander, that is the 6th century BC. The name by which the Zoroastrians call their own religion is Mazdayasna, the religion of Ahura Mazda (Sanskrit *Asura Medha*, "Lord of Wisdom"). The Rigveda 8.6.10 has the expression *medhām ritasya*, "wisdom of truth."

Zarathushtra presented his religion as rival to the religion of the *daevas*, or *Daevayasna*. Zarathushtra came from Bactria in northeast Iran, near Afghanistan. The Avesta speaks of several lands that include the Sapta-Sindhu (Sindhu-Sarasvati region of North and Northwest India). The Avesta includes the Yasna (Sanskrit *Yajna*) with the Gathas of Zarathushtra, Videvdat or Vendidad (*Vi-daeva-dat*, "anti-Daeva"), and Yasht (hymn), which are hymns for worship. During the Sasanian period the Avesta was translated into Pahlavi and this version is the Zend Avesta.

The Zoroastrians speak of mathra (Skt. *mantra*) as utterances that accompany meditation. Like the Vedic tripartite division of society, the Zoroastrians have the classes priests (zaotar), warriors (nar), and pasturers (vastar).

It has been assumed for some time that the daevas of the Mazda faith are the same as the Vedic devas and therefore Zarathushtra inverted the deva-asura dichotomy of the Vedic period. In reality, the situation is more complex and the Vedic and the Zarathushtrian systems are much less different than is generally supposed.

From Kashmir, which belongs square within the Vedic world, comes crucial evidence regarding a three-way division consisting of devas, asuras, and daevas. The scheme reflects the three-way division of Vedic thought that is also mirrored in the three gunas: sattva, rajas, and tamas.

Deva (heavens, sattva): power related to understanding

Asura (atmosphere, rajas): power related to activity

Daeva (earth, body, tamas): power related to acquisitiveness

Kashmiri folklore has many tales where daevas are counterpoints to devas and asuras. Sometimes the term *rakshasa* is used as a synonym for daeva. This term rakshasa occurs very frequently in Sanskrit literature, appearing in the Rigveda, the Aitareya Brahmana and other texts. (The rakshasa form of marriage is the violent seizure or rape of a girl after the defeat or destruction of her relatives.)

It is entirely possible that the term daeva came into Kashmir late as a result of the immigration of Persians. If that were the case, the reason why it took root is because it served as a synonym for an existing idea. It is equally possible that the term has been current in Kashmir from ancient times and its usage there parallels that by Zarathushtra from the nearby Bactria. Further support for this view comes from the fact that the Kashmiri Hindus, who have remained isolated from any Persian immigrations of the last few centuries, follow many practices that are prescribed for Zoroastrians. These include the sacred thread for women (called *aetapan* in Kashmiri) and the sacred shirt (*sadr*).

The Vedic view of seeing the world in triple categories was in the later Puranic gloss simplified into dichotomies like that of deva versus asura (including rakshasa). Zarathusthra made a similar simplification using the dichotomy of asura (including deva under the label yazata) and daeva. The asuras are the ground on which the devas emerge. The Zarathushtrian reduction is not particularly different from the Puranic.

Here I summarize the general structural and nomenclatural similarities between the Zoroastrian and the Vedic systems. I hope to show that the Zoroastrian innovations on the prior Vedic system in Iran have parallels in the adaptations that were taking place in India in the Puranic period. But Zarathushtra's emphasis on a sharp dichotomy between good and evil gave rise to an aesthetic and an approach that was quite unique. Below is a list of divinities that are included by the Zoroastrians amongst the forces of the good where I provide the corresponding Sanskrit spelling within brackets:

The Great Lord

The supreme God of the Zoroastrian faith is Ahura Mazda (Asura Medha). He is self-created, omniscient, omnipresent, holy, invisible, and beyond human conceptualization. In Yasht 1, Ahura Mazda proclaims: "My sixth name is Understanding; my seventh is Intelligent One; my eighth name is Knowledge; my ninth is Endowed with Knowledge; my twentieth is Mazda (Wisdom). I am the Wise One; my name is the Wisest of the Wise." This is reminiscent of Purusha in the Vedas.

The Cosmic Purusha projects on the three planes of the heavens, the sun, and the earth into the Vishve Devah, Indra, and Agni. Likewise, Ahura Mazda projects his power of good through the Amesha Spenta (Immortal Energy).

> Vohu Manah (Su Manah): Good Intention; Persian Bahman
>
> Asha Vahishta (Rta Vasishtha): Best Law; Ardvahisht
>
> Kshathra Vairya (Kshatra Vairya): Heroic Dominion
>
> Spenta Armaiti (Spanda Aramati): Bounteous Devotion
>
> Haurvatat (Sarvatva): Wholeness
>
> Amaratat (Amaratva): Immortality

The first three are are conceived of as masculine beings, the last three as feminine. The division of the six Amesha Spentas in three classes, with masculine and feminine forms, appears to parallel the projection of the power of Purusha into divinities in the three planes of Mind, Law, and Kingship.

Common Deities (Yazatas)

Many deities are identical in the Zoroastrian and the Vedic systems. Some can be recognized by noting the peculiar sound transformation in going from Sanskrit to Avestan such as *asha* obtained from *rita*.

Just as the Vedic deities are conceived within the framework of the bandhu between the astronomical, the terrestrial, and the physiological and the spiritual, the conception behind the Adorable Gods (Yajatas) includes several stars such as the Pleiades, Sirius, and Vega.

> Airyaman (Aryaman): An Aditya who appears together with Mitra. In Yast 3, there is invocation to *Airyama ishyo*, the "Desirable Airyaman." Aryaman represents hospitality.

> Apas (Apah): Cosmic Waters; Aban

> Apam Napat: Child of the Waters. The pre-Zoroastrian Varuna is still invoked in the yasna service as Apam Napat.

> Aradvi Sura Anahita (Sarasvati Shura): also Harahvati and the goddess Anahita

> Arshtat (Rita): Justice, Order

> Ashi, Maza-rayi (Maha-rayi): Fortune, "treasure-laden" (Yasht 17)

> Asman (Ashman): Stony vault, Sky; seen in opposition to Zam, Earth

> Atar (Atharvan): Agni

> Atharvan (Atharvan)

> Cista (Shishta): Goddess of the Way, Mithra's companion (16th Yasht)

> Daena: Religion, in later Persian Deen, "Woman who can possess you." The word *daena* survives in Kashmiri and Punjabi

> Dadar (Data): Giver

> Gav (Gauh): Cosmic Cow, Earth

> Hvar (Svar) : Sun; in later Persian the prefix Khor as in Khordad (given by Sun)

> Iza (Ida or Ila): Goddess of Sacrifice

Mithra (Mitra), also Mihr. Seen in Raman Khrashtra, "Rama's Kshatra," Ramarajya, in the Ram Yasht. Good Vay (Vayu) is called Ram (signifying joy and peace).

Sraosha (Brihas-pati): Companion of Mithra. In later Persia, as Sarosh or Siroos, he is the angel who mediates between God and man.

Thworeshta (Tvasta): Fashioner

Ushah (Usha): The Goddess Dawn that makes self-illumination possible

Vad (Vata): Wind

Vayu, Vay (Vayu): Breath

Verethraghan (Vritrahan): Indra as destroyer of the veil of ignorance (Vritra) as in the Vedas = Persian Bahram

Vivanhvant (Vivasvant): Sun

Yima (Yama); as in Jam or Jamshed (Yima Khshaeta, "Yima Radiant") deserted by Khvarnah (Suvarnah), Sun.

Mitra and Bhaga are two of the Adityas, names of the Sun, in the Vedas. The other Adityas from a late list are Indra, Aryaman, Vivasvant, Vishnu, Parjanya, Varuna, Dhatr, Pushan, Amshu, and Tvashta.

Since Mitra and Varuna are dvandva partners in the Vedas, the omission of Varuna from the Zoroastrian lists indicates that Zarathushtra was from the borderlands of the Vedic world where the Vedic system was not fully in place. This would also explain the omission of divinities such as Vishnu and Rudra. Likewise, it explains why the names of the Pleiades (Krittika in Sanskrit) are very different: Paoiryaeni.

But since Varuna is mentioned in the Mitanni documents, it is clear that the pre-Zoroastrian religion in Iran included Varuna.

It is remarkable that Baga (Skt. Bhaga), the pre-Zoroastrian name of God in Iran, is not listed amongst the Yazatas. This omission may be a consequence of the adoption of a new divinity, Ahura Mazda, in place of the old one.

Common Cultural Concepts

The Zoroastrian innovations did not change the basic Vedic character of the culture in Iran. The worship ritual remained unchanged as was the case with basic conceptions related to divinity and the place of man. In disease, the Zoroastrians speak of Aeshma in place of Yakshma.

Amesha (Amrita): Immortal. The emphasis is on a state beyond time from which the phenomenal world emerges.

Arta (Rita): Asha; Cosmic Order

Azi (Ahi): Dragon. This is the dragon that covers truth.

Baresman (Barhi): grass strewn on vedi

Druj (Druh): opposite of asha, falsehood, anrita

Framayishn (Yajamana)

Frashasti (Prashasti)

Hamkar (Samskara)

Haoma (Soma); used in ritual

Humayi (Su+maya): good maya

Karapan (Kripan): niggardliness, Zarathusthra is hostile to it

Kav, Kay, Kavi (Kavi): inspired seer

Mahal (Mahalaya)

Nahn (Snana): ritual bath

Pavi (Pavitra): place to sacrifice

Saena (Shyena): the eagle; also Saena meregh (mriga), Simurgh

Sogand (Saugandha): oath

Urvar (urvar): the original plant or productive ground; later Persian ruvan, soul

Vah, Vah (Svaha, Svaha): invocation at the fire ritual

Varah (Vrata): vow

Yasna (Yajna); also Jashn; the act of worship; sacrifice

Yatu (yatu): magic; jadu

Yima son of Vivanhvant (Yama son of Vivasvant)

Yazata (yajata); worthy of worship

Zaotar (hota): priest

Zaothra (Stotra): worship

The struggle between the Arya and the Dasyu in the Vedas is paralleled by one between the Arya and the Turya (Turks).

Five Divinites in Yasna Haptanhaiti

Ashi (Ashi): Reward, called Maza-rayi (Maharayi)

Ish (Isha): Enjoyment

Azuiti (Ahuti): Plenty

Frasasti (Prashasti): Satisfaction

Parandhi (Purandhi): Nourishment

Zarathushtra nowhere names the daevas born of Angra Mainyu (Pahlavi Ahriman, Hostile Spirit) but Middle Iranian books label Indar (Indra), Nanhaithya (Nasatya), and Savol. These appear to be a personification of the acquisitive aspects of the devas. Confirmation of this idea comes from the fact that Vayu in the Zoroastrian view is said to have two aspects, one good and another harmful (zinake). The good Indra, as Verethraghan (Vritrahan), the destroyer of the veil of ignorance, is a yazata.

Further Parallels

The list of common deities and concepts will make it clear that the Zoroastrian system is essentially the same as the Vedic one. The presence of Indra in the list of the daevas seems to mirror the relegation of Indra that started in the Puranic times where instead of connecting to Svar through the intermediate region of which Indra is lord, a direct worship of the Great Lord (Vishnu or Shiva) was stressed. This innovation is not counter to the Vedic system since the triple division is a recursive order. The devas are a part of the good forces in the Zoroastrian system under the label of yazata (yajata, the adored-ones).

The Zoroasatrian mythology remembers the Vedic sages and heroes such as Kavi Sushravah (Kay Khosrau), Kavi Ushanas (Kay Us). The names Kshatra Virya (Shahriyar) and Suvarnah (Khwarrah, Farrah) help find the logic of late Persian names. The daeva in modern Persian are known as deev.

The commonality of the fire ritual is well known. Less known is the ritual of the nine-nights (*barashnom i no-shab*) which is like the Indian ritual of the same name (*navaratri*).the No Roz occurs on the day of the spring equinox just as the festival of Indra.

Zarathushtra made a clear distinction between the good way (ashavant) and the false way (dregvant). The pre-Zoroastrian religion of Iran is clearly Vedic. Zarathushtra's innovation lay in his emphasis on the dichotomy of good and bad. But in details it retained the earlier structure of the Vedic divinities and their relationship as well as the central role of the fire ritual.

Evolution, Purity

The Pahlavi texts distinguish between the states related to the spirit and the body as menog (Skt. manas) and getig (Skt. gathita). The idea of Consciousness being primary is expressed in the theology as the creation first of menog and then getig. In the beginning both these are perfect but later due to "mixture" there is trouble. In general, evolution proceeds from the menog to the getig state. This is similar to the evolution from sattva to tamas.

The Pahlavi word for "confession" is patit which is identical to Sanskrit patita, fallen. Purification is done by yozdathra, shuddhi.

Herodotus states that the "Persians built no temples, no altars, made no images or statues" (Herodotus 1.131-2). Arrian in the Indica (7) says that Indians "did not build temples for the gods." To the outsider also, the two religions of the Persians and the Indians looked similar.

We already have evidence on the presence of the Vedic religion in West Asia in the second millennium BC. These ruling groups represented a minority in a population that spoke different languages. Other Vedic religion worshiping groups were undoubtedly in the intermediate region of Iran which itself consisted of several ethnic groups including the Elamite and the Turkic.

Zarathushtra brought a new element into the picture from the northeast. Linguistically, he happened to be "h" speaking in opposition to the Indic "s" speaking as in *haptah* versus *saptah* for week, or *hvar* versus *svar* for the Sun. He also brought the categorization of good versus evil onto the framework to create a new structure which was to be influential in the shaping of the Judeo-Christian tradition.

The old Vedic religion survived for a pretty long time in corners of Iran. The evidence of the survival of the devas comes from the daiva-inscription of Khshayarshan (Xerxes) (ruled 486-465 BC) in which the revolt by the daiva worshipers in West Iran is directly mentioned:

> Proclaims Khshayarshan the King: When I became king, there is among these countries one which was in rebellion. Afterwards Ahuramazda bore me aid. By the favor of Ahuramazda I smote that country and put it down in its place.
>
> And among these countries there was a place where previously daiva were worshiped. Afterwards, by the of Ahuramazda I destroyed that sanctuary of daiva, and I made proclamation: 'The daiva shall not be worshiped!' Where previously the daiva were worshiped, there I worshiped Ahuramazda at the proper time and in the proper manner. And there was other business that had been done ill. That I made good. That which I did, all did by the favor of Ahuramazda. Ahuramazda bore me aid until I completed the work.

Many believe that the use of daiva in the inscription as a misprint for daeva. Whether that is true or not, the inscription does point to the presence of diverse beliefs within the region during the middle of the first millennium BC. Furthermore, the presence of the Mitanni does support the notion of the daiva worshipers to the West of the Iranians.

The extensive spread of the Vedic religion in Iran prior to Zarathushtra explains how the Zoroastrian "reform" left the basic system unchanged. The similarities in the ritual offering made by the Zoroastrians and the Hindus are well known. These offerings include the milk, water, the sap of plants, cakes of rice or wheat, fruit and vegetables, butter.

The spread of the Vedic system also explains how the Mitannis, as an Indic-name using ruling minority, remained connected to their Vedic traditions. They were neighbors to the pre-Zoroastrian Vedic Iran and thus they should not be seen as an isolated group.

The chronological framework presented by the parallels between the Zoroastrian and the Vedic systems is in consonance with the idea that the Vedic people have been in India since at least 5000 BC, as confirmed by the astronomical references in the Vedic texts and the absence of archaeological evidence regarding influx of people into India after that time. The Puranas speak of the Vedic people in Jambudvipa and beyond the Himalayas in the north in Uttara-Kuru. It appears that subsequent to the collapse of the Sarasvati-river based economy around 1900 BC, groups of Indians moved West and that might have been responsible for the Aryanization of Iran if it wasn't Aryanized earlier. This movement seems to be correlated with the presence of the Indic Kassites and the Mitannis in West Asia.

In such a scenario, the Uttara-Kuru tribes, who were a part of the larger Vedic world, may have pushed Westwards in a process that must have continued for millennia and taken myths from the Indic region to Europe. This was not a process of invasions but rather a complex process with some migration and some cultural diffusion. One should note that about 10,000 years ago most of northern Europe was under ice in the last Ice Age and the inhabitants of ice-free southern Europe were speakers of non-Indo-European languages such as the Basque, Etruscan and Finnish of later times. To the extent the Uttara-Kuru tribes moved West, they must have intermarried with local populations to emerge as different European tribes.

The divergence in the names of the stars, which were central to the Vedic ritual, suggests that there existed variation in the traditions, reflecting local custom and influence of other cultures.

If the tradition of Zarathushtra being 258 years before Alexander is correct, then the syntheses of Zarathushtra and the Buddha, one extolling wisdom (medha) and the other intelligence (buddhi), occurred at almost the same period. The use of temples is late in the Zoroastrian and the Hindu traditions and it may have been a response to the popularity of the Buddha image and the sangha that administered it.

16

The Mitanni

A sad consequence of the colonialist historiography of the 19th century Indologists is the comparative neglect of India's interaction with Africa. Cyril Hromnik's *Indo-Africa* (1981) is the only book on the Indian contribution to the history of sub-Saharan Africa that I am aware of, but it is just an exploratory study. The story of India's interaction with Egypt is better known, if only to scholars. Two important figures in this story are the Mitanni king Tushratta and the New Kingdom pharaoh Akhenaten. But even this encounter between the Indoaryan speaking Tushratta and the Egyptian Pharaoh is not well understood although it was to have far-reaching implications for world history.

The Sun King Akhenaten of Egypt (ruled 1352-1336 BC according to the mainstream view) was a son-in-law of Tushratta, the Mitanni king of North Syria, through queen Kiya. (The name Tushratta is spelled Tuishrata in the Hittite cuneiform script, which does not distinguish between "d" and "t" very well. Some have suggested that the Sanskrit original is Dasharatha, a few others that it is Tvesharatha (having splendid chariots), a name which is attested in the Rigveda. Letters exchanged between Akhenaten and Tushratta have been found in Amarna in Egypt and other evidence comes from the tombs of the period, which have been discovered in excellent condition.

The Amarna age is one of the best-known and most romantic periods of ancient Egypt. Akhenaten was revolutionary in his religious beliefs, and many argue that his ideas mark the beginnings of the Western monotheistic tradition. This period also saw the fabulously beautiful Nefertiti, Akhenaton's first queen who came from a mixed Mitanni family, palace intrigues, artistic triumph and great personal tragedy.

Here I investigate the question whether the worship of the Sun introduced by Akhenaten might have had connections with the Indic beliefs of the Mitannis. Implications of this early encounter between the Indic and the Western worlds will also be examined in view of the widely accepted opinion amongst biblical scholars that Akhenaten's beliefs were the model for the later Jewish and Christian beliefs.

The Mitanni, who worshiped Vedic gods, were an Indic kingdom that had bonds of marriage across several generations with the Egyptian 18th dynasty to which Akhenaten belonged. The Mitanni were known to the Egyptians as the Naharin (N'h'ryn'), connected to the river (nahar), very probably referring to the Euphrates. At its peak, the Mitanni empire stretched from Kirkuk (ancient Arrapkha) and the Zagros mountains in western Iran in the east, through Assyria to the Mediterranean sea in the west. Its center was in the region of the Khabur River, where its capital, Wassukkani was probably located.

The first Mitanni king was Sutarna I (good sun). He was followed by Baratarna I (Paratarna, great sun), Parashukshatra (ruler with axe), Saustatar (Saukshatra, son of Sukshatra, the good ruler), Paratarna II, Artadama (Ritadhaman, abiding in cosmic law), Sutarna II, Tushratta (Dasharatha), and finally Matiwazza (Mativaja, whose wealth is thought) during whose lifetime the Mitanni state appears to have become a vassal to Assyria.

The early years of the Mitanni empire were occupied in the struggle with Egypt for control of Syria. The greatest Mitanni king was Saukshatra who reigned during the time of Tuthmose III. He was said to have looted the Assyrian palace at Ashur. Under the reign of Tuthmose IV, more friendly relations were established between the Egyptians and the Mitanni.

The daughter of King Artadama was married to Tuthmose IV, Akhenaten's grandfather, and the daughter of Sutarna II (Gilukhipa) was married to his father, Amenhotep III, the great builder of temples who ruled during 1390-1352 BC ("khipa" of these names is the Sanskrit kshipa, night). In his old age, Amenhotep wrote to Tushratta many times wishing to marry his daughter, Tadukhipa. It appears that by the time she arrived Amenhotep III was dead. Tadukhipa was now married to the new king Akhenaten, becoming famous as the queen Kiya (short for Khipa).

The Egyptian kings had other wives as well. Akhenaten's mother, Tiye, was the daughter of Yuya, who was a Mitanni married to a Nubian. It appears that Nefertiti was the daughter of Tiye's brother Ay, who was to become king himself. The 18th dynasty had a liberal dose of Indic blood, a consequence of the westward movement of Indians after about 1900 BC.

We see Kassites, a somewhat shadowy aristocracy with Indic names and worshiping Surya and the Maruts, in Western Iran about 1800 BC. They captured power in Babylon in 1600 BC, which they were to rule for over 500 years. The Mitanni, another group that originated thus, ruled northern Mesopotamia (including Syria) for about 300 years, starting 1600 BC, out of their capital of Vasukhani. (For Mitanni names, I give standard Sanskrit spellings rather than the form that we find in inscriptions in the inadequate cuneiform script, such as Wassukkani for Vasukhani, "a mine of wealth"). Their warriors were called marya, which is the proper Sanskrit term for it.

In a treaty between the Hittites and the Mitanni, Indic deities Mitra, Varuna, Indra, and Nasatya (Ashvins) are invoked. A text by a Mitannian named Kikkuli uses words such as aika (eka, one), tera (tri, three), panza (pancha, five), satta (sapta, seven), na (nava, nine), vartana (vartana, round). Another text has babru (babhru, brown), parita (palita, grey), and pinkara (pingala, red). Their chief festival was the celebration of vishuva (solstice) very much like in India. It is not only the kings who had Sanskrit names; a large number of other Sanskrit names have been unearthed in the records from the area.

Documents and contract agreements in Syria mention a warrior caste that constituted the elite in the cities. The ownership of land appears to have been inalienable. Consequently, no documents on the selling of landed property are to be found in the great archives of Akkadian documents and letters discovered in Nuzi. The prohibition against selling landed property was dodged with the stratagem of "adopting" a willing buyer against an appropriate sum of money.

Information of the mythology of the Hurrians of the Mitanni is known from related Hittite and Ugaritic myths. The king of the gods was the weather god Teshub who had violently deposed Kumarbi paralleling the killing of Vritra by Indra. Major sanctuaries of Teshub were located at Arrapkha (modern Kirkuk) and at Halab (modern Aleppo) in Syria. Like Indra, Teshub also had a solar aspect. In the east his consort was the goddess of love and war Shaushka (Venus), and in the west the goddess Hebat (Hepat). In addition, a considerable importance was attributed to impersonal gods such as heaven and earth as well as to deities of mountains and rivers. Temple monuments of modest dimensions have been unearthed.

The general Indic influence in the area may also be seen in the comprehensiveness of the god lists. The most "official" god list, in two Ugaritic copies and one Akkadian translation, consists of 33 items, exactly as is true of the count of Vedic gods. These gods are categorized into three classes, somewhat like the three classes of the Vedic gods, although there are difference in details.

Greek accounts tell us that the Ugaritic believed in a cosmic egg out of which the earth emerged which is reminiscent of the Vedic view.

How do we know that the Mitanni were Indic and not Iranian? There are several reasons, but to be brief, I shall only give three: 1. the deities Indra, Mitra,

Varuna, and Nasatya are Indian deities and not Iranian ones, because in Iran Varuna is unknown and Indra and Nasatya appear as demons; 2. the name Vasukhani makes sense in Sanskrit as a "mine of wealth" whereas in Iranian it means "good mine" that is much less likely; 3. satta, or sapta, for seven, rather than the Iranian word hapta, where the initial 's' has been changed to 'h'.

Why could not the Mitanni be the descendents of a pre-Vedic people from Central Asia? They would then have had no particular affinity for Indic deities. If the pre-Vedic people in Central Asia already had Indian deities, how would these small bands of people impose their culture and language over what was perhaps the most densely populated region of the ancient world. Furthermore, that view does not square with our knowledge of the astronomical tradition within India. The Vedic Samhitas have very early astronomical and its geography is squarely within India. The earlier texts remember events within the Indic geographical area going back to the third and the fourth millennia BC. The theory of a proto-Indoaryan people in Iran from whom the Aryans of India descended in the second millennium BC does not work for the same reasons.

Indic Names in West Asia

Over fifty years ago, Roger T. O'Callaghan and W.F. Albright published in *Analecta Orientalia* of Rome a list of 81 names (13 from the Mitanni, 23 from the Nuzi, and 45 from the Syrian documents) with Indic etymologies. Out of this list, Dumont provided the etymology of 45 names in the much more readily available *Journal of the American Oriental Society* of 1947. A few of these names with the Sanskrit cognates in parentheses are:

Abirata (Abhirata, pleased, contented)

Aitagama (Etagama, with the gait of an antelope)

Aitara (the son of Itara)

Artamanyu (Ritamanyu, revering the divine Law)

Ardzawiya (Arjaviya, straight, honest)

Birasena (Virasena, possessing an army of heroes)

Biridashwa (Brihadashva, possessing great horse)

Bardashwa (Varddhashva, the son of Vriddhashva)

Bayawa (Vayava, the son of Vayu)

Biryashura (Viryashura, the hero of valor)

Biryawadza (Viryavaja, owning the prize of valor)

Biryasauma (Viryasoma, the moon-god of valor)

Birya (Virya, valor)

Indarota (upheld by Indra)

Kalmashura (Karmashura, the hero of action)

Purdaya (Purudaya, giving much)

Ruchmanya (Ruchimanya, revering light)

Satuara (Satvara, swift)

Shaimashura (Kshemashura, the hero of security)

Subandu (Subandhu, being good kinsmen)

Sumala (having beautiful garlands)

Sumida (Sumidha, bountiful)

Swardata (Svardata, given by heaven)

Tsitriyara (Chitrya-rai, having distinguished property)

Uruditi (having wide splendour)

Warasama (Varasama, equal to the best)

Wasasatta (Vasasapta, possessing seven dwellings)

Wasdata (Vasudata, given by the Vasus)

Yamiuta (Yamyuta, favoured by Yamin)

Analyzing the names, Dumont concludes that the names are clearly Indic and not Iranian. The initial "s" is maintained and the group "shv" is represented by the similar sounding "shw" and not the Avestan "aspo." Also, most of the names are *bahuvrihi or tatpurusha* compounds.

Considering the language, it is clearly an Indic dialect because the initial "v" is replaced by "b", while medial "v" becomes the semivowel "w". Like Middle Indic (Prakrit) dialects, the medial "pt" transforms into "tt," as in *sapta* becoming *satta.*

Dumont stresses its relationship to Sanskrit in the characteristic patronymic names with the *vriddhi*-strengthening of the first syllable as in Saumati (the son of Sumati). The worship of the Vedic gods like Indra, Vayu, Svar, Soma, Rita, Vasus has already been noted.

The fact the the Mitanni names suggest a Middle Indic dialect is supportive of the thesis that the emigration of the various groups from India took place after the early Vedic period had come to an end.

Akhenaten's Rule

Akhenaten ("glory of the Aten") ascended the throne as Amenhotep ("Amun is content") IV but he changed his name to honor Aten ("One god" represented as the solar disk) in his sixth regnal year. Aten is the deification of the disk of the sun god, Ra, who was also represented by the eye.

Akhenaten moved his capital from Thebes to Akhetaten ("Horizon of Aten"), now known as Amarna, where palaces and buildings were built from mud brick, and in which he built a splendid temple to Aten filled with religious art.

After his father's death, he built temples on the perimeter of the famous Temple of Amun at Karnak and dedicated them to Aten, rather than Amun ("the Hidden One," the principal deity at the time, also known as Amen). He erased the names of other gods, particularly Amun, and he also erased his father's name wherever he found it.

Some argue that Akhenaten introduced monotheism by the banishment of all deities excepting his chosen one. He has been seen as a precursor to the Old Testament prophets, and thus to the Abrahamic religions. But it is equally plausible that he was influenced by the belief in "One Truth" behind appearances of the Vedic system through the three generations of queens in his family from the Mitannis.

The importance of the Vedic element appears to be reflected in the mysticism of the Egyptian Book of the Dead (from 1600 BC on). Nevertheless, the cult of the dead and resurrection remained the most important element of the Egyptian religion. This cult continues to form the cornerstone of the three Abrahamic faiths.

Akhenaten was succeeded by Smenkhkara, believed by some to be Nefertiti herself, and soon afterwards by Tutankhaten, Akhenaten's son by Tadukhipa (Kiya) under the regentship of Ay. Akhenaten was a fanatic and the country had suffered a great deal during his reign. The nobles now reversed course. Tutankhaten changed his name to Tutankhamen (to invoke Amun), but before he could consolidate power he was dead at the age of sixteen after a rule of just nine years. His tomb was discovered intact in 1922, and now he is widely known as the Boy-King.

Tutankhamen was followed by Ay, Nefertiti's father, who ruled for four years. He, in turn, was followed by the general Horemheb, who now erased all records of Akhenaten, and his successors. The new city was abandoned, and worship of the Amun was reestablished. Akhenaten's disappeared from Egyptian history, and he was referred to as "that heretic" or "rebel," until the reconstruction of the history in modern times. Yet, his idea of a jealous god lived on, and prospered.

Letters, Religion, and the End of Tushratta

The context to the Amarna correspondence, in which there are letters between the Egyptian, Mitanni, and other neighboring kings, is now available. These diplomatic letters, totalling nearly 400, were written in a space of about thirty-five years from about 1370 to 1335, from the end of the reign of Amenhotep III to the death of Tutankhamen. The texts were written in a dialect known as Western Peripheral Akkadian which was the lingua franca of the Near East, though one letter from Tushratta, is written in Hurrian.

Here is an extract from a letter by Tushratta to Amenhotep III, Akhenaten's father: "My father loved you, and you loved my father still more. And my father, because of his love, has given my sister to you … Behold, one chariot, two horses, one male servant, out of the booty from the land of Hatti I have sent you. And as a gift for my brother, five chariots and five teams of horses I have sent you. And as a gift for Gilukhipa, my sister, one set of gold pins, one set of gold earrings, one gold idol, and one container of sweet oil I have sent her." Another letter accompanies the image of goddess of Shaushka of Nineveh (Ishtar), sent to Amenhotep III to restore him to health during illness. Ishtar is Venus, and the Vena hymn of the Rigveda (10.123) anticipates her Mesopotamian mythology.

A message of greetings from Tushratta to Akhenaten: "To Napkhuria (Akhenaten), king of Egypt, my brother, my son-in-law, who loves me and whom I love, thus speaks Tushratta, king of Mitanni, your father-in-law who loves you, your brother. I am well. May you be well too. Your houses, Tiye your mother, Lady of Egypt, Tadukhipa, my daughter, your wife, your other wives, your sons, your noblemen, your chariots, your horses, your soldiers, your country and everything belonging to you, may they all enjoy excellent health."

The Vedic presence via the Mitanni in Egypt and West Asia occurs several centuries before the exodus of the Jews. This presence is sure to have left its mark in various customs, traditions, and beliefs. Small Indic groups remained in the general area for centuries after the disappearance of the Mitanni. Thus Sargon defeats one Bagdatti of Uishdish in 716 BC. The name Bagdatti (Skt. Bhagadatta) is Indic and cannot be Iranian because of the double "t."

It may be that the continuing encounter between Indic and West Asian groups explains some parallels in mythology and ritual, such as worship of the goddess, circumambulation around a rock or the use of a rosary of 108 beads. This encounter was facilitated by the trade that continued between these two regions of Asia. There is ample evidence for this trade during the Harappan period and earlier. Harappan objects have been found in numerous places in West Asia. Weights of the highly accurate Harappan system, which was different from the one in use in Mesopotamia, have been found in Dilmun in West Asia. It is likely that such trade continued in the second and first millennia BC.

In the Amarna Letters, the correspondents are from Egypt, Mitanni, Babylonia, Hatti, and Assyria. Mitanni was also called Hanigalbat and Naharin; Babylonia is also named Karaduniyash or Shanhar; Hatti (of the Hittites) was sometimes named after its capital of Hattusha. In the Letters, Amenhotep III is called Mimmureya or Nimu'wareya or Nibmureya, while Akhenaten is also called Naphurureya.

The Hittite king Suppiluliumas launched a surprise attack on the Mitanni kingdom. In the course of his victorious march, Mitanni began to crumble and Tushratta was assassinated. His son fled through various lands, returning at long last to Vasukhani as a vassal. Mitanni as an independent kingdom ceased to exist. As the vassal of the Hittites, the rump state was called Hanigalbat. Soon afterward, it was captured by the Assyrian Adad-nirari I (probably during the reign of

Horemheb) and later by Shalmaneser I (during the reign of Ramesses II), at which time the area east of the Euphrates was turned into an Assyrian province.

In 1937, Freud published his essay, "Moses and Monotheism," in the journal *Imago* proposing that the biblical figure of Moses was an Egyptian linked to the court of Akhenaten. Freud provided much stimulating evidence to support his argument, including the fact that the Jewish word for "Lord," "Adonai," becomes "Aten" when its letters are written in Egyptian.

The other details of Freud's reconstruction are disputed but they are significant for estimating the importance of the Egyptian ideas within the Judeo-Christian tradition. According to Freud, Moses was a believer in the monotheism associated with Aten, but with the death of Akhenaten the successor Pharaohs reverted to their old religion. Moses (from *mose*, Egyptian for "child") now went to exile as the head of an oppressed Semitic tribe and in order to set these people apart, he introduced the Egyptian custom of circumcision. His unruly followers killed Moses, and the tribesmen now adopted the volcanic deity, Yahweh of another tribe, as their national god. Yahweh was now endowed with the universal and spiritual qualities of the Moses's god, though the memory of Moses's murder remained repressed amongst the Jews, reemerging in a very disguised form with the rise of Christianity.

There is general agreement that Moses—who is said to have lived a staggering 120 years—was a composite character created out of the faded memories of a variety of different individuals, some Hebrews, others Egyptian in origin. The Egyptian component included the memory of Akhenaten's worship of the single god in the sky.

According to Freud, the death of Moses became central to the experience of the Jews and it defined the structure of Christianity as well. Says Freud: "Original sin and salvation through sacrificial death became the basis of the new religion founded by Paul. After the Christian doctrine had burst the confines of Judaism, it absorbed constituents from many other sources, renounced many features of pure monotheism, and adopted in many particulars the ritual of the other Mediterranean peoples. It was as if Egypt had come to wreak her vengeance on the heirs of Ikhnaton [Akhenaten]. The way in which the new religion came to terms with the ancient ambivalency in the father-son relationship is noteworthy. Its main doctrine, to be sure, was the reconciliation with God the Father, the expiation of the crime committed against him; but the other side of the relationship manifested itself in the Son, who had taken the guilt on his shoulders, becoming God himself beside the Father and in truth in place of the Father."

Within the Indo-Iranaian world, the memory of India's interaction with Egypt persisted. In Chapter 48 of his book on India written in 1030, al-Biruni, speaking of chariots of war, mentions the Greek claim that they were the first to use them and insists they are wrong because "they were already invented by Aphrodisios the Hindu, when he ruled over Egypt, about 900 years after the deluge." This reference cannot be taken to be literally true but it is, nevertheless, significant. It preserves the memory of a "Hindu" (Indic-inspired) king of Egypt prior to the Greek state. The reference to the chariots of war of this king (Akhenaten) seems to remember the foreigner warlords Hyskos who ruled Egypt during the Second Intermediate Period just before the New Kingdom to which Akhenaten belonged.

17

Yahvah and Yehweh

History can be a great friend in times of crisis. Consider the ongoing sexual molestation and homosexuality crisis of the Catholic Church. Looking back into the Church history one finds that celibacy was adopted only a few centuries ago. The medieval popes were princes. Anyone fond of Italian history would recall the Medicis and the Borgias, in particular, Pope Alexander VI and his beautiful daughter Lucrezia. Many bishops in early Christianity were married, as were 39 Popes. Celibacy was introduced to ensure that the organization of the Church did not lose power to any one family. It was sold wrapped in the theological formula that each priest was to be married to the Church and each nun to Christ. The Church can easily abrogate this theology, claiming connection to an older tradition.

History helps in understanding current religious questions by explaining the original meaning of words and lending perspective. It is essential for regeneration and renewal because it lets one see the context in which certain ideas and practices arose.

Consider the general belief that East and West are forever apart because their religions originated in different circumstances. Is there no commonality between the two? I argue in the last chapter that the idea of monotheism for Akhenaten was derived from his Mitanni (Indic) queen, Tadukhipa. But can we go any further than speculation and speak of textual reference in support of the idea?

El and Yahweh

The Abrahamic religions trace their lineage to El and Yahweh. The Jewish and Christian God is called YHWH in Hebrew and spelt as Yehweh or Yahvah. According the Huston Smith's book *The World's Religions* (p. 222): "Allah is formed by joining the definite article 'al' meaning 'the' with 'Ilah' (God). Literally, Allah means 'The God.' … When the masculine plural ending im is

113

dropped from the Hebrew word for God, Elohim, the two words sound much alike." Eloah (Hebrew feminine) is similar to Ilah (God).

What is the origin of the Ila and Yahweh? El was the chief god of the Phoenicians and the Ugarits. Yet El is also the name used in many Psalms for Yahweh. In 2 Kings 22:19-22 we read of Yahweh meeting with his heavenly council. The Ugaritic texts have a similar account, with the difference that the "sons of god" are the sons of El. Other deities worshipped at Ugarit were El Shaddai, El Elyon, and El Berith. Since all these names are applied to Yahweh by the writers of the Old Testament, we can be sure that the Hebrew theologians assimilated the earlier mythology into their system.

Besides the chief god at Ugarit there were also lesser gods and goddesses. The most important of the lesser gods were Baal, the goddess Asherah, Yam (the god of the sea) and Mot (the god of death); Yam and Mot are the Hebrew words for sea and death, respectively. Asherah, a very important character in the Old Testament, is called the wife of Baal, although she is also known as the consort of Yahweh. Inscriptions dated between 850 and 750 BC say: "I bless you through Yahweh of Samaria, and through his Asherah!" And at 'El Qom (from the same period) this inscription: "Uriyahu, the king, has written this. Blessed be Uriyahu through Yahweh, and his enemies have been conquered through Yahweh's Asherah." The Elephantine Papyri tells us that the Hebrews worshiped Asherah until the 3rd century BC.

Baal's name occurs frequently in the Old Testament. Some Israelites viewed Yahweh as a God of the desert and so when they arrived in Phoenicia they thought it only proper to adopt Baal, the god of fertility. One of the central Ugaritic myths is the story of Baal's enthronement as king. In the story, Baal is killed by Mot and he remains dead until the new year. His victory over death was celebrated as his enthronement over the other gods.

The idea of an annual ritual death was widespread in the ancient world and it had a solar basis. The death and regeneration was taken to occur on the winter solstice, to celebrate the beginning of the new year. The Old Testament also celebrates the enthronement of Yahweh. As in the Ugaritic myth, the purpose of Yahweh's enthronement is to re-enact creation. Yahweh overcomes death by his recurring creative acts.

The major difference between the Ugaritic myth and the Biblical hymns is that Yahweh's kingship is eternal and uninterrupted while Baal's is interrupted every year by his death. Since Baal is the god of fertility the meaning of this myth is quite easy to understand. As he dies, so the vegetation dies; and when he is reborn so is the world. Not so with Yahweh; since he is always alive he is always powerful.

When one reads the Psalms of the Old Testament and the Ugaritic texts one finds that Yahweh is acclaimed for things previously associated with El. These Psalms appear to have been originally Ugaritic or Phoenician hymns to El which were adopted by the Jews. El is called the "father of men" "creator," and "creator of the creation," attributes also granted Yahweh by the Old Testament.

Ila and Yahvah

The different Semitic gods have cognates in the Vedic pantheon. Yam may be connected to the Vedic Yama who in RV 10.10.4 is seen as being born from the waters, and Mot to the Vedic Mrityu, death. But more to the point, Ila represents Agni as in Yajurveda (VS) 2.3, whereas Ilaa represents Earth, speech, and flow. There is also the Vedic Yahvah. As an epithet it is associated with movement, activity, heaven and earth; it means the sacrificer and Agni, the chief terrestrial god. It is associated with energy like the Yahwah of the Semites. The name Yahvah occurs 21 times in the Rigveda. It may be compared to Shivah, an epithet for auspiciousness in the Rigveda, that later is applied regularly to Rudra.

Are Ila and Yahvah like El and Yahweh just by coincidence? We don't know, but we certainly do know of the Vedic-god worshiping Mitanni of North Syria who could have served as the intermediaries in connecting the Indians and the Semites.

Ila and Yahvah are not better known in India because names in themselves are not central to the Indic system. The essence of the Vedas is that God is a category beyond words and one may describes its aspects by a variety of names. This is the reason there are 3 names (the triplicity arising from the three-fold division of the inner and the outer universes), or 33 names, or 330 million names of God. It is remarkable that the god lists of the Ugarits also contain 33 names.

It would be foolish to deduce that if Yahvah and Yahweh are identical names then the Vedas become the source of the Abrahamic traditions or Christianity the fulfillment of the Vedas. The Indic gloss on the matter is that names in themselves are mere sequence of syllables and they mean nothing; it is not names but the way of seeing reality that matters. The Western and Indian spiritual traditions as they exist now are quite different and they represent the unique genius of each region. But perhaps the commonality of origin could help people see the universality of the spiritual quest and help build bridges across cultures in these difficult times.

18

The Tree of Knowledge

The tree of knowledge may answer our wishes, but its foliage is so dense that one can get lost in it. The Upanishads tell us that the gods love what is paradoxical (*paroksha*) and detest what is straightforward (*pratyaksha*). Not surprisingly, the Upanishads also tell us that those who worship only the material end up in darkness, and those who worship only the spirit end up in greater darkness.

The path of wisdom is a narrow path. The pulsations of reality may be subtle, but appearances are structured. Great scientists, who work at the frontier of their field, are aware of the limitations of academic knowledge and are aware of its transitory nature. But most ordinary scientists are no more open-minded than religious zealots.

When I was a boy, I heard my father tell me about his extraordinary experience during his years of spiritual quest. He mentions some of these in his fragmentary autobiography, *Autumn Leaves*. I didn't know what to make of his stories. I wanted to believe my father, but I was also skeptical. In the end, I decided to seek my answers through science.

My research has focused on different aspects of information; this eventually led me to quantum theory. It was good to see that, at its deepest, science asked as many questions as it answered. I was also interested in grammar, linguistics and machine translation and before long I confronted the magnificent grammar of Panini.

The ancient rishis were incredibly prescient and creative. A lot of what they said is still relevant. After all, their main concern was consciousness, precisely what modern science is trying to understand.

This takes us back to yoga—the union of our ordinary awareness with our true self. The promise of Indian wisdom is the realization of our potential. This is done through yoga as a discipline that complements the way of looking at the outer world through academic science. We get gleanings of the spark within by learning to observe ourselves.

The universe is woven together and interconnected. The symbol of the interconnectedness of the physical universe is the invisible axis around which the stars move; likewise, the unity of our experience is established by the axis of consciousness to which we bind our associations.

We are so used to the routine of the everyday that we become oblivious to the extraordinary nature of our commonest experience. It is not just the coming of new life that is magical; every experience when our senses are truly open is magical. The dance of Shiva happens not only at the cosmic level, it occurs also at each moment, and as one grain of time is gone and dead, the next grain comes along and there is new creation!

There lie many adventures in the path to the unfolding of the mystery of self. Each human being is a scientist and historian of sorts: we reason and gather knowledge; we structure all that happens around us. If it all doesn't add up, we must step back and wonder.

Mind is the last frontier of science. We observe the physical universe through our mind, yet we have no clear idea how mind functions, how memories are stored and recalled and what the origin of our subjective feelings is. Is this level of ignorance a result of the reductionist nature of the tools that have been used in the study of mind and consciousness? If that is so, will an approach that has a different philosophical basis help? It is for this reason we turn to the Vedas, where the central concern is self and awareness.

The Vedic texts consider reality to transcend the duality of matter and mind. This non-dual reality, this Brahman, is present in all material manifestations, but is best understood as the knowing subject within us. The space of this knowledge is consciousness. Later literature, self-consciously describes itself as dealing with the nature of consciousness.

The texts, speak of the cognitive centers as individual, whole entities which are, nevertheless, a part of a greater unity. The vocabulary used in these texts challenges the modern reader, but once one has learned the definitions of the operative terms, the structure soon becomes apparent. Vedic mythology is often an explication of understanding of consciousness, and so mastering the Vedic vocabulary provides us a means of unlocking the hidden meaning behind the myths.

In the Vedic discourse, the cognitive centers are the devas—deities or gods, or luminous loci. The Atharvaveda (10.2.31) calls the human body the city of the devas. This passage also speaks of the body consisting of eight cognitive centers which, other references suggest, are hierarchically organized.

The devas are visualized in a complex scheme, with some being closer to the autonomous processes of the body and others being nearer creative centers. In analogy with ordinary space, inner space of consciousness is viewed to have three zones: the body (earth), the exchange processes (prana, atmosphere), and the inner sky (heavens). The number of devas is variously given, one extravagant passage counts 3.3 million. The Brihadaranyaka Upanishad (3.9.1) remembers a hymn that praises 3306 of them, arguing there are 33 major deities, distributed in three groups of eleven among the three zones. All these devas are taken to embody the same light of consciousness. The mind consists of discrete agents, although it retains a unity.

Since each deva reflects primordial consciousness, one can access the mystery of consciousness through any specific deva. Thus there is a deva for reading and learning, one for recognition, one for friendship, one for generosity, and so on. Physics and the Vedas agree that reality is consistent only in its primordial, implicate form. The Vedas insist that speech and sense-associations cannot describe this reality completely.

In quantum physics we have similar insights. The use of ordinary logic leads to paradoxes such as an entity can be simultaneously present at more than one place, and the present can influence the past! At a less technical level we may ask: How do we reconcile the determinism of science to the subjective sense of free will?

Modern discoveries that are based on a study of consciousness states and the deficits caused by lesions, stroke, injury, or surgery that disrupts the normal functioning of our senses and cognitions appears to uphold the Vedic view. These discoveries suggest that the mind is a complex structure of various localized functions held together by a unitary awareness. The most recent findings appear to confirm ancient intuitions.

India has a glorious past, but that, in itself, is no reason to do anything more than acknowledge it, and move on. The more interesting reason for our fascination with India is the possibilities it offers to the modern man, curious to know the nature of his self. India's insights are astonishing yet they are not inconsistent with science. They offer a way to integrate modern science with a science of self. It is for this reason that we return to this tradition, and for this reason alone that this tradition will eventually be embraced everywhere.

Notes

[1] H. Zimmer, *Myths and Symbols in Indian Art and Civilization*. Princeton, 1946.

[2] T.B. Macaulay wrote his Minute in 1835. He was a central figure in the language debate over which language should be used as the medium of education in India. The Orientalists favoured the use of classical languages of Indian tradition, such as Sanskrit, Persian and Arabic, which were not spoken as native languages. The Anglicists, on the other hand, supported English. The objective of both schools was the furtherance of the British empire in India.

[3] E. Schrödinger, *Meine Weltansicht*. Vienna, 1961; see also W. Moore, *Schrödinger: Life and Thought*. Cambridge, 1989.

[4] Moore, *op cit.*

[5] Moore, *op cit.*

[6] E. Schrödinger, *What is Life?* 1944, p. 87.

[7] Schrödinger, *op cit*, p. 89.

[8] S. Kak, *The Astronomical Code of the Rgveda*, Delhi, 2000; G. Feuerstein, S. Kak, D. Frawley, *In Search of the Cradle of Civilization*. Wheaton, 1995, 2001.

[9] V.S. Wakankar, "Rock painting in India." In *Rock Art in the Old World*, M. Lorblanchet (ed.), New Delhi, pp. 319-336.

[10] S. Oppenheimer, *The Real Eve: Modern Man's Journey out of Africa*, New York, 2003.

[11] J.-P. Vernant, in M. Olender, *The Languages of Paradise: Race, Religion, and Philology in the Nineteenth Century*. Cambridge, 1992.

[12] Vernant, *op cit.*

[13] Olender, *op cit.*

[14] N.S. Trubetskoy (1939) quoted in C. Renfrew, *Archaeology and Language: The Puzzle of Indo-European Origins.* London, 1987, page 108.

[15] Renfrew, *op cit.*

[16] M.B. Emeneau, *Language and Linguistic Area.* Stanford, 1980.

[17] D. Napier, "Masks and metaphysics in the ancient world: an anthropological view." Presented at the *International Seminar on Mind, Man and Mask,* Indira Gandhi National Centre for the Arts, New Delhi, Feb 24-28, 1998.

[18] J.P. Mallory, *In Search of the Indo-Europeans.* London, 1989.

[19] E. Leach, "Aryan invasions over four millennia." In *Culture through Time, Anthropological Approaches,* E. Ohnuki-Tierney (ed.), Stanford, 1990, pp. 227-245.

[20] Ohnuki-Tierney, *op cit.*

[21] Lalita Pandit, "Caste, Race, and Nation:History and Dialectic in Rabindranath Tagore's *Gora.*" In *Literary India: Comparative Studies in Aesthetics, Colonialism, and Culture.* Patrick Colm Hogan and Lalita Pandit (eds.). Albany, 1995.

[22] J.G. Shaffer and D.A. Lichtenstein, "Ethnicity and change in the Indus valley cultural tradition." *In Old Problems and New Perspectives in the Archaeology of South Asia,* J.M. Kenoyer (ed.), Wisconsin Archaeological Reports, vol. 2, Madison, 1989.

[23] J.G. Shaffer and D.A. Lichtenstein, "Migration, philology and South Asian Archaeology." In *Aryan and Non-Aryan in South Asia: Evidence, Interpretation and Ideology.* J. Bronkhorst and M. Deshpande (eds.), Ann Arbor, 1999.

[24] M. Kenoyer, *Ancient Cities of the Indus Valley Civilization.* London, 1998.

[25] M. Danino, *The Invasion That Never Was.* Delhi, 2000.

[26] P.T. Srinivas Iyengar, "Did the Dravidians of India obtain their culture from Aryan immigrant?" *Anthropos,* vol. 9, 1914, pp. 1-15.

[27] R. Swaminathan Aiyar. *Dravidian Theories.* Madras, 1975.

[28] C. Geertz, *Negara: The Theatre State in 19th Century Bali.* Princeton, p. 104.

[29] N. Kazanas, "The Rgveda and Indo-Europeans," *Annals of the Bhandarkar Oriental Research Institute,*vol. 80, 1999, pp. 15-42.

[30] D. Napier, *op cit.*

[31] O. Alvarez, *Celestial Brides: A Study in Mythology and Archaeology.* Stockbridge, 1978.

[32] T. Taylor, The Gundestrup cauldron. *Scientific American,* vol. 266 (March), 1992, pp. 84-89.

[33] S. Kak, "The solar equation in Angkor Wat," *Indian Journal of History of Science,* vol. 34, 1999, pp. 117-126. F.G. Millar and S. Kak, "A Brahmanic fire altar explains a solar equation in Angkor Wat," *Journal of the Royal Astronomical Society of Canada,* vol. 93, 1999, pp. 216-220.

[34] A. Boner, "Introduction" In *Śilpa Prakāśa,* A. Boner, A. and S. Rath Śarmā, (eds.). Leiden, 1966. pp. xxxiii.

[35] B.L. van der Waerden, "Two treatises on Indian astronomy." *Journal for History of Astronomy,* vol. 11, 1980, pp. 50-58.

[36] K.M. Ganguly (ed.), *The Mahabharata.* Delhi, 1990, vol.9, page 23.

[37] E.C. Sachau, *Alberuni's India.* Delhi, 1989.

[38] W. Caland, *Pañcavimśa Brāhmana.* Calcutta, 1982, page 440.

[39] P.N. Mathur, "Decipherment of Indus script and traditional Indian history." In *New Trends in Indian Art and Archaeology.* B.U. Nayak and N.C. Ghost (eds.). New Delhi, 1992.

[40] S.Kak, The *Astronomical Code of the Rgveda,* Delhi, 2000

[41] C.G Jung, *Psychological Types.* Princeton, 1971, pp.12-13.

[42] J.M. Keynes, quoted in G. de Santillana and H. von Dechend, *Hamlet's Mill.* Boston, 1969.

[43] J.D. Palmer, *An Introduction to Biological Rhythms.* New York, 1976

[44] A. Coomaraswamy, *The Dance of Shiva.* New York, 1985

[45] Quoted in H.G. Rawlinson, "Early contacts between India and Europe." In A.L. Basham (ed.), *Cultural History of India*. Oxford, 1975.

[46] H.G. Rawlinson, *op cit.*

Index

978-0-595-48699
0-595-48699-1

Made in the USA
Middletown, DE
27 November 2022